Electronic Discovery for Small Cases

Bruce A. Olson and Tom O'Connor

Managing Digital Evidence and ESI

ABA **LawPracticeManagementSection**
MARKETING • MANAGEMENT • TECHNOLOGY • FINANCE

Commitment to Quality: The Law Practice Management Section is committed to quality in our publications. Our authors are experienced practitioners in their fields. Prior to publication, the contents of all our books are rigorously reviewed by experts to ensure the highest quality product and presentation. Because we are committed to serving our readers' needs, we welcome your feedback on how we can improve future editions of this book.

Cover design by ABA Publishing.

Printed in the United States of America.

16 15 14 13 12   5 4 3 2 1

Library of Congress Cataloging-in-Publication Data

Olson, Bruce A.
   Electronic discovery for small cases : managing digital evidence and ESI /
Bruce A. Olson and Tom O'Connor.
      p. cm.
   Includes bibliographical references and index.
   ISBN 978-1-61438-350-5 (alk. paper)
   1. Electronic discovery (Law)—United States. 2. Electronic records—Law and legislation—United States. 3. Digital signatures—Law and legislation—United States. 4. Electronic evidence—United States. I. O'Connor, Tom. II. Title.
      KF8902.E42O47   2012
      347.73'72—dc23

                                                                    2012011266

Contents

About the Authors

Bruce A. Olson is president of ONLAW Trial Technologies, LLC, a legal technology consulting firm offering services in the areas of computer forensics, electronic trial and litigation support management, and e-discovery and electronic records management. Mr. Olson is a lawyer licensed in the state of Wisconsin. Prior to assuming a full-time consulting practice, Mr. Olson was a shareholder in the Wisconsin-based law firm of Davis & Kuelthau, S.C., working from its Green Bay and Milwaukee offices. He is an experienced trial lawyer, having practiced for almost thirty years in the areas of commercial and business litigation, employment litigation, computer and technology related litigation, product liability litigation, professional liability defense, and environmental litigation.

Mr. Olson has extensive experience dealing with e-discovery, electronic records and data management, and related legal and trial presentation computer technologies. He is AV rated in Martindale-Hubbell and is a board certified civil trial advocate, having been certified by the National Board of Trial Advocates in 1997 and recertified in 2002 and 2007. He has tried over sixty jury trials to verdict in either the federal district courts or the circuit courts of Wisconsin, and has handled appeals at the Wisconsin Court of Appeals, the Wisconsin Supreme Court, and the Seventh Circuit Court of Appeals. In June of 2010, Mr. Olson received his Certified Computer Examiner (CCE) designation from the International Society of Forensic Computer Examiners.

Mr. Olson is also a nationally recognized legal technologist focusing primarily on the areas of computer forensics, e-discovery, and litigation technology. He is the co-author of *The Electronic Evidence and Discovery Handbook: Forms, Checklists and Guidelines*, published by the American Bar Association's Law Practice Management Section. He was the recipient of the prestigious TechnoLawyer of the Year 2002, awarded by the Techno-Lawyer community. He was chair of ABA TECHSHOW 2004, vice chair of ABA TECHSHOW 2003, and served on the ABA TECHSHOW Board of Directors from 2000–2004. He has been a frequent and highly rated speaker at the ABA TECHSHOW, at various LegalTech presentations, and at state bar-sponsored presentations throughout the United States. He has published technology-related articles on Law.com and in *Digital Forensics Investigator News*, *TechnoLawyer*, *Law Office Computing*, *Law Technology News*, *Law Firm Governance*, and other national publications.

Tom O'Connor is a nationally known consultant, speaker, and writer in the area of computerized litigation support systems. He is a New England native who graduated from the Johns Hopkins University in 1972 with a BA in political science. After attending law school for one year at the University of Notre Dame, Tom returned to Baltimore and undertook a career as a paralegal specializing in complex litigation.

Over the years he has worked on asbestos litigation, the *Keating* cases, the San Diego Civic Center construction litigation, California class actions against crematoriums, national breast implant litigation, tobacco litigation on behalf of the attorney general of Texas, and various phases of the Enron litigation. More recently, Tom has expanded his practice to include electronic document depositories, trial presentation systems, and e-discovery.

A frequent lecturer on the subject of legal technology, Tom has been on the faculty of numerous national CLE providers and on the advisory board of the ABA TECHSHOW and the American Lawyer Media Legal Tech conferences. A prolific writer with articles in numerous legal publications, as well as editing several legal newsletters, Tom is the author of *The Automated Law Firm: A Complete Guide to Software and Systems,* published by Aspen Law & Business, and *The Lawyers Guide to CT Summation iBlaze, Second Edition,* published by the American Bar Association's Law Practice Management Section.

Sometime over the past twenty years, Tom also found time to return to law school and earn a JD. He and his best friend Gayle, along with their son Seamus, the philosopher king of Western Washington University, hope someday to have their own float in a Mardi Gras parade down the Mississippi down in New Orleans, where Tom now resides.

Acknowledgments

THE AUTHORS WOULD LIKE to acknowledge the contributions and assistance from the following people: Megan Miller from Digital WarRoom Pro; Elizabeth Thede of dtSearch Corporation; Gene Albert of Lexbe; Rakesh Madhava and Laura Waldman of Nextpoint; Rick Borstein of Adobe; Matthew Knutson of Quick View Plus; Jonathan Rowe of Pinpoint Labs; Peter Mercer of Intella; Tim Johnson of the American Bar Association Law Practice Management Section; and David Ries, our project manager.

Tom O'Connor would like to thank Seamus, for constantly reminding him what is really important in life, and Gayle, who showed him how to live again. You have often been a headache, babe, but you have never been a bore.

Introduction

WITH THE HIGH NUMBER of electronic discovery (e-discovery) vendors and conferences, Webinars, seminars, and online training venues, you might ask why this book is necessary. Indeed, when we spoke on the subject at the 2011 ABA TECHSHOW, we did not expect much of a turnout. The room was packed, however, and we both realized we had struck a nerve.

Why? We call it the "small case dilemma." We will explore the small case dilemma below, but first we will give you a quick overview of e-discovery and how we got to where we are now. Then we will look at some of the products that have sprung up to answer the small case dilemma and talk about where we think this field is going in the next few years.

To begin with, however, we would like to make a general observation. Very few large e-discovery vendors were willing to talk about this subject on the record. This was not surprising to us because such companies traditionally have ignored the small case market. Now, with the economy in turmoil, competition for work is intense, large vendors are buying smaller companies, and many consultants and service bureaus with multiple vendor contracts are reluctant to jeopardize those deals by voicing an opinion that might be perceived as criticism.

On the other hand, many companies that target the small case market were highly cooperative in discussing their products, and we appreciate their assistance. Please keep in mind, however, that the opinions in this book are ours unless otherwise directly noted. Not that we do not have strong opinions. In the words of our good friend Browning Marean, senior counsel at DLA Piper, we are "often wrong, but never uncertain."

How to Use This Book

When writing books about e-discovery, it is difficult to know what level of understanding your reader brings to the book. Some are new to the topic and need generalized knowledge before they turn to more specific technical information. Others are experienced and want to skip the general discussion and jump directly to the technical portions of the book. Consequently, we have written the book in two parts.

The first part is intended to give a general overview of e-discovery, particularly in the context of smaller cases. It is intended to be introductory in nature and more general in scope.

The second part presents different scenarios one likely will encounter in dealing with e-discovery in smaller cases. Specific software solutions are offered in considerable detail to provide a sense of the types of products that are available to address your particular needs. Needs vary depending on the nature of the case, where you are in the e-discovery process, and the size of your technology budget. We cannot write about every software product on the market, or the book would never end. Our goal is to introduce you to a variety of products at varying price points that are capable of accomplishing specific tasks to help you develop your own strategies for dealing with e-discovery in smaller cases.

This is a book about technology. As a result, technical terms are used throughout. In order to provide accurate information, it is necessary at times to use technical terms with which you may not be familiar. We have tried to explain the terms in the context of the book as much as possible. However, to the extent there are terms that are not adequately explained, we refer the reader to the glossary at the end of the book. For more detailed information, we recommend two additional sources for definitions: The Sedona Conference Glossary is available at **http://www.thesedonaconference.org**, and the EDRM Glossary is available at **http://www.edrm.net/resources/glossary**.

PART ONE

Electronic Discovery Overview

CHAPTER ONE

Rule Changes

FORMALIZED CHANGES TO THE Federal Rules of Civil Procedure regarding e-discovery went into effect in December 2006, but discussions about the use of electronic documents in litigation had been underway long before that. In the late 1980s, U.S. Senate investigators in the Iran-Contra affair were able to retrieve 758 e-mail messages sent by Oliver North regarding his involvement in the operation. North had believed the e-mail messages to be deleted. He was subsequently convicted of lying under oath to a congressional committee.

Roughly ten years later, then vice president Al Gore's fundraising activities were under investigation by the U.S. Department of Justice. White House Counsel Beth Norton eventually reported that it would take up to six months to search through 625 storage tapes of White House e-mail.

Thus, the American Bar Association adopted the Civil Discovery Standards in 1999, which included provisions addressing preservation duties and cost shifting in relation to e-discovery. Those standards were cited thereafter in a number of federal cases, most notably Judge Shira A. Scheindlin's decision in *Zubulake v. UBS Warburg*.[1]

Throughout the *Zubulake* case, the plaintiff claimed that the evidence she needed to prove her position existed in e-mails stored on UBS Warburg's own computer systems. Because the e-mails requested were either never located or destroyed, the court found that it was more likely than not that they had, in fact, existed. The court also found that, although the defen-

---

[1] 216 F.R.D. 280, 283 n.30 (S.D.N.Y. 2003).

dant corporation's counsel directed that all potential discovery evidence, including e-mails, be preserved, the staff, to which this directive applied, did not follow through on the instructions. The result was significant sanctions against UBS Warburg.

By March of 2000, a long period of review and debate began in earnest. The Committee on Rules of Practice and Procedure of the Judicial Conference of the United States appointed an Advisory Committee on the Rules of Civil Procedure, which was tasked with monitoring the effectiveness of the rules and making recommendations for proposed amendments. Given that amendments to the Federal Rules of Civil Procedure have been passed only nine times (in 1948, 1963, 1966, 1970, 1980, 1983, 1987, 1993, and 2000), the process was a serious undertaking. The recommended e-discovery changes eventually were approved by the U.S. Supreme Court and went into effect in December of 2006.

During this same time period, the Sedona Conference, a nonpartisan law and policy think tank, published the first edition of *The Sedona Principles: Best Practices Recommendations and Principles for Addressing Electronic Document Production.* This document was also influential in the eventual recommendations of the advisory committee. The second amended version of *The Sedona Principles* was released in July of 2007.

After the Federal Rules of Civil Procedure amendments were enacted, many states also changed their rules to follow and, in some cases, mirror the changes to the federal rules. At the time of this writing, over two-thirds of the states have established e-discovery rules. The most up-to-date information on state rules can be found in a list compiled by Thomas Y. Allman, former senior vice president, general counsel, and chief compliance officer of BASF Corporation and, subsequently, senior counsel to Mayer, Brown, Rowe & Maw. Allman was an early advocate of the amendments to the Federal Rules of Civil Procedure to achieve e-discovery reform and a leader in the formulation of *The Sedona Principles.* His list can be found at **http://www.fiosinc.com/case-law-rules/e-discovery-state-rules-civil-procedure.aspx**.

The result of all these rule changes has been to effectively force civil litigants into compliance mode with respect to their retention and management of electronically stored information (ESI). The risks that litigants face as a result of improper management of ESI include findings of spoliation of evidence, summary judgment findings, and the award of sanctions, including adverse inferences, adverse jury instructions, and even complaints filed by judges with state bar associations. For more on this issue, see the detailed opinions in *Qualcomm Inc. v. Broadcom Corp.*[2] and *Pension Committee of the University of Montreal Pension Plan v. Banc of America Securities, LLC.*[3]

---

[2]539 F. Supp. 2d 1214 (Jan. 26, 2007).
[3]685 F. Supp. 2d 456 (S.D.N.Y. Jan. 15, 2010, as amended May 28, 2010).

CHAPTER TWO

E-Discovery— The Early Years

Types of ESI

The Federal Rules of Civil Procedure were revised in the 2006 amendments not to define ESI, but to identify it as a separate category of discoverable information. In fact, there is no formal definition of ESI in the rules, although Rule 34(a)(1)(A) does provide that a party may serve on any other party a request within the scope of Rule 26(b) to produce "any designated documents or *electronically stored information—including writings, drawings, graphs, charts, photographs, sound recordings, images, and other data or data compilations—stored in any medium* from which information can be obtained either directly or, if necessary, after translation by the responding party into a reasonably usable form . . . ." (emphasis added).

Examples of the type of data included in e-discovery are word processing documents, spreadsheets, e-mail, accounting databases, CAD/CAM files, Web sites, instant messaging, text messaging, chat room conversations, voice mail systems, and any other ESI that could be relevant evidence in a lawsuit. Also included in e-discovery is raw data, which forensic investigators can capture and collect for later review by lawyers. This might include data that has been deleted, intentionally or not, as well as data preserved by the computer in temporary files, slack space, computer and network activity logs, cache and temporary Internet files, or other locations not apparent to a user.

Reasonably Accessible

The Federal Rules of Civil Procedure impose an obligation to identify data that is potentially relevant and reasonably accessible, as well as data that might be relevant but not accessible. This is an important distinction because the duty to preserve and the duty to produce are not interchangeable. Put another way, simply because data is not reasonably accessible and thus cannot be easily produced does not mean it can be destroyed.

Amended Rule 26(b)(2)(B) provides that ESI need not be produced if the source is not reasonably accessible because of undue burden or undue cost. Constantly evolving changes in technology make this a shifting definition. For example, at the time of the 2006 amendments, legacy backup tapes were considered inaccessible, but technological improvements in tape retrieval since 2006 have made that definition much less definitive.

Merely asserting that data is inaccessible is not a sufficient explanation. Judges likely will require detailed cost estimates to support such assertions and often request alternative estimates from neutral vendors when they think the cost claims are excessive.

When the court finds that the requested information is relevant, unavailable elsewhere, or crucial to the matter at hand, it may override the undue cost burden argument and order production. In that case, the court likely will entertain arguments for cost sharing or shifting.

Native Formats

Amended Rule 34 allows the requesting party to specify the form or forms of production. If the requesting party does not specify the form, the producing party must indicate the form in which it intends to produce. The producing party may also object to the requested form, but in either case it must produce ESI in the form in which it is "ordinarily maintained or . . . a reasonably usable form or forms . . . ."[1] The original file format is known as the "native" format.

The Advisory Committee note on this point is most instructive. "A party that responds to a discovery request by simply producing electronically stored information in a form of its choice, without identifying that form in advance of the production in the response required by Rule 34(b), runs

---

[1]FRCP Rule 34(b)(2)(E).

a risk that the requesting party can show that the produced form is not reasonably usable and that it is entitled to production of some or all of the information in an additional form."[2]

If the ESI ordinarily is maintained in a searchable format, the notes make it clear that it may not be produced in a form that "removes or significantly degrades this feature." In simple terms, this most commonly means that taking e-mail or spreadsheets and printing them out or converting them to a PDF destroys the searchable native format, rendering them not "reasonably usable" and, therefore, not responsive.

Handling ESI: EDRM

The Electronic Discovery Reference Model (EDRM) Project was initiated in 2005 by e-discovery experts and consultants George Socha and Tom Gelbmann. The project was created to address the lack of standards and guidelines in the e-discovery market.

The initial goal of the EDRM was to provide a common framework for the development, selection, evaluation, and use of e-discovery products and services. The completed reference model as shown in Figure 2.1 was placed in the public domain in May 2006 and provides an excellent visual tool for analysis and discussion of any e-discovery project, regardless of size.

Figure 2.1

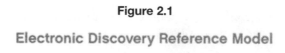

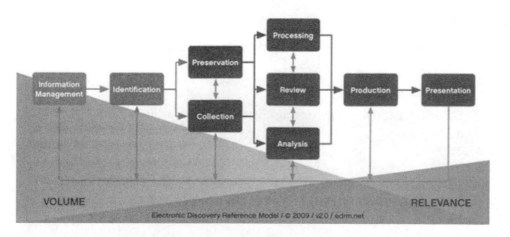

---

[2]Advisory Committee Note to Rule 34.

Since that time, EDRM has continued as an ongoing guidelines and standards body designed to educate about e-discovery challenges, vendors, and processes. It has provided two subset standards: EDRM Metrics, which is intended to provide a standard approach and a generally accepted language for measuring the full range of e-discovery activities, and EDRM XML, an XML schema to facilitate movement of electronic information from one step of the e-discovery process to the next, one software program to the next, and one organization to the next. A Model Code of Conduct standard is currently under development.

EDRM also continues to supply guidelines, standards, whitepapers, research materials, Webinars, news, data sheets, and other items to help educate e-discovery consumers and providers, all of which can be found on the EDRM Web site, **http://edrm.net**. We encourage you to familiarize yourself with the EDRM and its commentary to develop the necessary skills to practice effectively in this area of the law.

Workflow

The EDRM has been most helpful in identifying the specific stages of handling ESI in the discovery process. The EDRM's definition of the stages is as follows:

Information Management

Getting your electronic house in order to mitigate risk and expenses should e-discovery become an issue, from initial creation of electronically stored information through its final disposition.

Identification

Locating potential sources of ESI and determining its scope, breadth and depth.

Preservation

Ensuring that ESI is protected against inappropriate alteration or destruction.

Collection

Gathering ESI for further use in the e-discovery process (processing, review, etc.).

Processing

Reducing the volume of ESI and converting it, if necessary, to forms more suitable for review and analysis.

Review

Evaluating ESI for relevance and privilege.

Analysis

Evaluating ESI for content and context, including key patterns, topics, people, and discussion.

Production

Delivering ESI to others in appropriate forms and using appropriate delivery mechanisms.

Presentation

Displaying ESI before audiences (at depositions, hearings, trials, etc.), especially in native and near-native forms, to elicit further information, validate existing facts or positions, or persuade an audience.[3]

Existing technologies have been used for years for many of these functions, including forensic collection tools, document management systems, full-text search engines, litigation databases such as Summation and Concordance, and tools and presentation systems ranging from PowerPoint to litigation-specific applications designed for use in the courtroom.

More recently, many of these existing applications have been modified to meet the challenges of handling ESI, and new products specific to this market are constantly appearing. The goal of all these products is to perform specific functions within the EDRM framework, whether the forensic capture of data, electronically processing that data to cull it down to a manageable amount of documents for review, or performing that review on a Web-hosted platform that allows multiple users in multiple locations to access the data at the same time.

A better example of this workflow process is captured in Figure 2.2.

---

[3]**http://www.edrm.net/resources/edrm-stages-explained**.

Figure 2.2

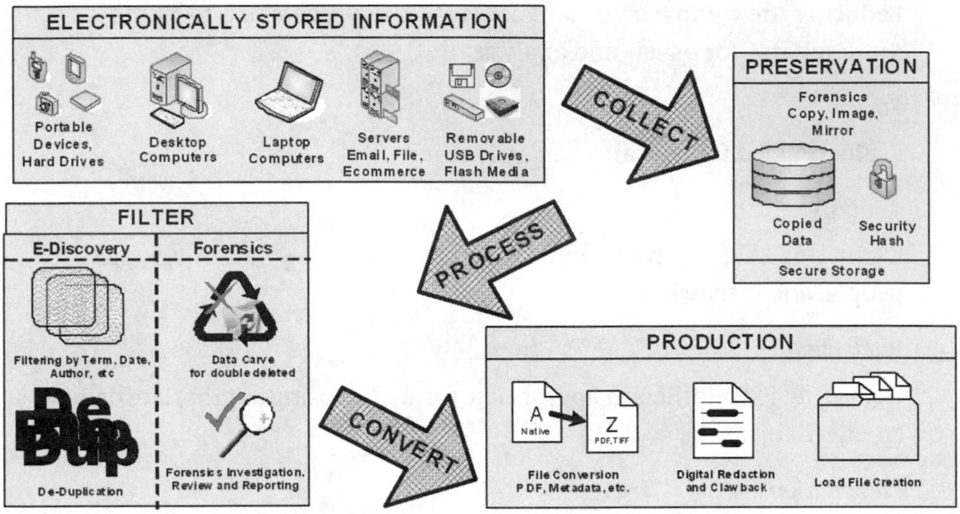

Sedona Cooperation Proclamation

On October 7, 2008, the Sedona Conference released its Cooperation Proclamation (SCP), which was publicly endorsed by over twenty judges, including the Honorable Judges Shira Scheindlin, Andrew Peck, Paul Grimm, David Waxse, and John Facciola, all leading jurists in the area of e-discovery. The SCP was designed to speed the reasonable, just, speedy, and less expensive approaches to e-discovery mandated by Rule 1 of the Federal Rules of Civil Procedure. To that end, it shifted the focus from discovery disputes to litigating on the merits.

Shortly after its publication, Judge Grimm extolled the focus of the SCP in *Mancia v. Mayflower Textile Services Co.*[4] *Mancia* was an employment litigation case in which the parties had reached a discovery impasse that did not even involve ESI. Judge Grimm wrote, however, that "[c]ourts repeatedly have noted the need for attorneys to work cooperatively to conduct discovery, and sanctioned lawyers and parties for failing to do so."

Judge Grimm went on to write that "[p]erhaps the greatest driving force in litigation today is discovery. Discovery abuse is a principal cause of high litigation transaction costs. Indeed, in far too many cases, economics—and not the merits—govern discovery decisions. Litigants of moder-

---

[4]2008 WL 4595175 (D. Md. Oct. 15, 2008).

ate means are often deterred through discovery from vindicating claims or defenses, and the litigation process all too often becomes a war of attrition for all parties."

He then set forth the essence of the SCP, observing that:

> . . . there is nothing at all about the cooperation needed to evaluate the discovery outlined above that requires the parties to abandon meritorious arguments they may have, or even to commit to resolving all disagreements on their own. Further, it is in the interests of each of the parties to engage in this process cooperatively. For the Defendants, doing so will almost certainly result in having to produce less discovery, at lower cost. For the Plaintiffs, cooperation will almost certainly result in getting helpful information more quickly, and both Plaintiffs and Defendants are better off if they can avoid the costs associated with the voluminous filings submitted to the court in connection with this dispute. Finally, it is obvious that if undertaken in the spirit required by the discovery rules, particularly Rules 26(b)(2)(C) and 26(g), the adversary system will be fully engaged, as counsel will be able to advocate their clients' positions as relevant to the factors the rules establish, and if unable to reach a full agreement, will be able to bring their dispute back to the court for a prompt resolution. In fact, the cooperation that is necessary for this process to take place enhances the legitimate goals of the adversary system, by facilitating discovery of the facts needed to support the claims and defenses that have been raised, at a lesser cost, and expediting the time when the case may be resolved on its merits, or settled. This clearly is advantageous to both Plaintiffs and Defendants.

For small cases, this approach is crucial. It means that the ultimate solution is more than just knowing the rules, avoiding e-jargon, and understanding the technology. The key is good lawyering and understanding the scope of *all* the procedural rules, not just those dealing with ESI. In fact, a good argument can be made that small cases require an even greater level of understanding of these factors than larger cases. With larger cases, you typically have bigger budgets and more room to make mistakes. In small cases, a targeted plan of attack must be developed from the outset that will be sufficiently thorough to provide relevant discovery, yet cost effective so the more limited budget will suffice.

CHAPTER THREE

Small Case Dilemma

IN 2010, NOTED E-DISCOVERY consultant Craig Ball wrote a fascinating article in *Law Technology News* titled "EDD for Everybody." That column came to be known as the "EDna Challenge" because in it Craig posited a solo practitioner named Edna with an e-discovery budget of $1,000 and asked how she could possibly perform any e-discovery on that amount.

The problem, as Ball defined it, was simple:

> The vast majority of cases filed, developed and tried in the United States are not multimillion dollar dust ups between big companies. The evidence in modest cases is digital, too. Solo and small firm counsel like Edna need affordable, user-friendly tools designed for desktop e-discovery—tools that preserve metadata, offer efficient workflow and ably handle the common file formats that account for nearly all of the ESI seen in day-to-day litigation.

Ball set the following goals for his challenge:

1. Preserve relevant metadata;
2. Incorporate de-duplication, as feasible;
3. Support robust search of Outlook mail and productivity formats;
4. Allow for efficient workflow;
5. Enable rudimentary redaction;
6. Run well on most late-model personal computers; and
7. Require no more than $1,000.00 in new software or hardware, though it's fine to use fully-functional "free trial" software so long as you can access the data for the 2–3 year life of the case.

He then solicited a wide-ranging number of answers from a variety of consultants and vendors and compiled them into the article, which can be found on his Web site at **http://www.craigball.com/E-Discovery%20 for%20Everybody.pdf**.

The problem of cases with budgets too low for most ED productions still exists, and that is the essence of our small case dilemma. Where are those programs? Is there really a way to process and review a couple of hundred gigabytes (GB) of data for a reasonable price? Are there really low cost but technically adept applications that lawyers can use to host and review that same data? If not, why?

Pricing

The first problem is current pricing in the market. Why is this? Because many, if not most, e-discovery vendors are rooted in the per-unit commodity pricing days of photocopying and imaging. The standard practice for years now has been to charge hundreds of dollars per gigabyte to process the data, which includes culling, deduping, and de-NISTing of the data set, then preparing it for loading into review software.

Once processing is done, the data is loaded into a hosting platform for review, and a second set of charges is incurred. These typically are both by gigabyte and user on a monthly basis, as well as some initial flat fees to "prepare" and load the data.

As a result, a simple license plus annual maintenance or a monthly subscription fee model for e-discovery products typically does not exist. Instead, we must sort through hundreds of products priced by varying and often widely divergent methods: $X per GB for processing, $X per page for OCR, $X per document for near duplicate detection, $X per page for Bates numbers, $X per user and per GB to host, and so on. Each is performed for different units with different unit pricing that can run from one penny to $500 per unit.

For example, if a client pays for a forensically sound data collection of 800 GB (the size of the hard drive of one typical computer), and that data set eventually yields 200 GB of reviewable material, a typical e-discovery company will charge $200 per GB for the processing ($160,000), plus $50 per month per GB ($10,000) and $90 per month per user for the hosting. If the case lasts eighteen months, this cost alone will be just under

$350,000. If we accept the commonly cited statistic that the review process will account for 60–70 percent of the total project price, then we are looking at a project cost that will eventually be close to $1,000,000 for 200 GB of data.

To avoid the shock of those costs being immediately apparent, vendors often use pricing sheets in response to an e-discovery RFP that look like the menu in a Chinese restaurant—without English subtitles. Very few people have the experience, let alone the patience, to sort through those sheets. In fact, we have been called by clients on many occasions to help them in that process because the separate bids they receive to an RFP do not even appear to respond to the same proposal!

If your case is worth only $400,000 and, after analysis and discussion with your client, you believe you cannot spend more than $10,000 for ESI processing and hosting services over the anticipated eighteen-month life of the case, you have a problem. If your case falls within the scope of the EDna Challenge, a small case with an e-discovery budget of less than $1,000, you have a very big problem.

Big Vendors and Big Products for Big Cases

As you might expect, at this low price point, traditional vendors simply have not been interested in 200 GB cases. Sales managers at two separate top-tier companies have told us directly that big ED companies do not want this business. Why? Because they cannot support themselves on small jobs. Large companies have large overhead and need large revenue amounts to support that infrastructure. These companies may have spent millions of dollars developing software or, more commonly, acquiring another company with its existing software. When this cost is added to their mindset of unitized pricing noted above, they are locked into a system of set monthly costs. From their perspective, they simply cannot give away their services to small firms with small cases.

Big Collections

In addition, the technology for e-discovery initially was developed for large cases with large data sets. Companies with revenue streams based on processing or hosting terabytes (TB) of data cannot easily adapt to projects consisting of several hundred gigabytes, much as you cannot expect a 747 jumbo jet to be used as an effective or cost-efficient means of transporting commuters during rush-hour traffic.

Big Products

Finally, products that have been designed to work with immense data collections cannot easily scale down to small sets of information. A Sequel-based product, such as the Microsoft SQL Server software or a relational database management system, working with terabytes of data on a distributed Internet framework needs a certain hardware and software infrastructure to operate. That type of system cannot be scaled down to load onto a laptop or an iPad. Big products have big prices, however, and both the products and the prices are beyond the scope of most small firms and small case budgets. Although those cases might be small to an international corporate service provider, however, they mean everything to the person involved in the lawsuit and the lawyers who represent them.

CHAPTER FOUR

A Cooperative Approach to Managing E-Discovery in Smaller Cases

GIVEN THE BACKGROUND SET forth in the previous chapters, what is the average practitioner to do to effectively manage e-discovery in small cases? There are some practical ways in which you can approach the issue that can help. The first thing you can do costs nothing apart from the time spent thinking as a good lawyer. It is probably the most important thing you can do to minimize costs. Take the time to think through what you really want in terms of discovery of ESI. Make your requests targeted and specific enough to elicit exactly what you need for your case. Too often lawyers use the all-encompassing approach of casting the widest net possible. This obviously magnifies the cost of discovery. It might be done as a strategy, but more often it is done because it is easier to do. Asking for everything does not require you to think about your case and determine early on what you need to meet your burden of proof. If you carefully tailor your requests, you can limit the amount of work that must be done and lessen the amount of data that must be processed and reviewed. You will also have a good argument to persuade your opposing counsel to do the same (or a judge in the context of a motion for a protective order), thereby lessening your client's costs in responding to e-discovery requests.

How do you go about performing effective triage at the outset? In federal court you have a great tool: the meet and confer. Many states have similar provisions in their state civil procedure laws. Our recommendation is meet early and meet often. Although there may be a mandatory requirement to have at least one meet and confer, you are not limited to only one meeting. If you meet early with your opposing counsel, you can take steps to define what they have, let them know how they should preserve it, and determine how it should be collected in the most cost-effective way possible. You can do the same for your client's ESI so you can minimize your own expense in terms of preservation and production concerns.

Next, know what you really want. If you are not concerned with deleted information, you probably do not need the help of a computer forensics expert. On the other hand, if you do need the help of a computer forensics expert, that determination should be made quickly, and collection efforts should occur as soon as possible to avoid the inadvertent loss of information due simply to the normal operation of computer systems. If you are not really concerned with metadata, you might be able to use less expensive collection options that do not preserve the metadata associated with the ESI you are collecting. You never want to make that decision in the dark, which is why the issue should be dealt with at a meet and confer. Still, often you are really only looking for a copy of a file and do not care about the metadata of the original. If you know what you are doing, and what you are giving up, you can minimize collection costs by stipulation. Even if you do need to preserve metadata, there are relatively inexpensive options available that you can use without hiring expensive outside consultants. It may take a higher level of technical ability on your part, and you must determine if you are comfortable engaging in self-collection methods, but there are lower cost options available. If you are comfortable, then you can negotiate with the other side to use appropriate software tools to collect the ESI that you must produce and that you want produced by your opponent.

One technique that can be considered at a meet and confer is the use of phased discovery. Why demand the ESI from every potential witness in a case when a more targeted approach might better serve your needs? Agree to limit initial collection efforts to the key custodians you want, and agree that if discovery of their ESI proves fruitful, you can move on to collection from other, more peripheral players. If e-discovery does not produce much of value with the key witnesses, you can safely skip the other witnesses.

Even with key witnesses, consider a phased approach by using sampling techniques. Before you demand production of an individual's full file shares from a company server, consider whether you should first review just the e-mail files from the e-mail server. If that analysis turns up attachments that are relevant, then you can move on to the file server. Limit the type of information you seek initially. If you are not looking for financial data, then do not demand production of all spreadsheet files. If there is a limited date range at issue, do not ask for every document on the server; ask only for those that fall within the pertinent date range. If you can limit the scope of what you are looking for by the use of key words, try filtering on key words. It might get you what you want right away. If key word searching is unsuccessful, you can then consider broadening the search or abandoning it altogether.

If you are a lawyer who does not have a great deal of experience in e-discovery, get some help—the earlier the better. Hiring a consultant who can help you develop a streamlined e-discovery plan may cost some money up front, but in terms of avoiding the cost of spinning your wheels or making mistakes, the overall expense will be lessened. Hire the right kind of consultant to help you. Vendor-neutral consultants typically do not have a vested interest in using one particular product or procedure. A vendor-affiliated consultant always has a biased agenda. The bias may be useful to your case, but be aware of what you are getting.

Planning, a targeted approach to discovery, cooperation between counsel, and the use of the proper tools to meet your specific case needs can help you lessen the cost of e-discovery in smaller cases. There are many practical technology options available short of a dedicated litigation support database solution to meet your needs in smaller cases. You must find what works best for you within the budget you have available and the particular ESI you must manage. Those options are the subject of Part Two of this book.

PART TWO

Technology Tools for Small Cases

CHAPTER FIVE

Collection Concerns— Should You Collect ESI by Yourself or Seek Outside Assistance?

HAVING DISCUSSED THE EVOLUTION of e-discovery and the particular concerns raised by smaller cases, it is time to look at available software tools that can help meet the challenges of the small case dilemma. The following chapters examine a number of different software products that can help during the different phases of e-discovery. The software is introduced to you in the context of common scenarios you are likely to encounter when dealing with e-discovery in smaller cases. Showing how given products can meet a particular need should help you in determining what type of tools you should use to meet a particular challenge. We do not intend these chapters to be exhaustive. There are other fine products out there that we have not covered in the book due to space constraints; new products are constantly developed. Our hope, however, is that an introduction to these products will give you a sense of what is available in the market and what the average lawyer can bring to bear to manage e-discovery in small cases in a cost-effective way.

One of the first tasks you will confront in conducting e-discovery in small cases is the collection of ESI from your client and possibly from the other side. This typically means the collection of active files, not deleted files. (If you seek deleted information in addition to active files, a computer forensics expert is required.) At first blush, this would seem fairly straightforward. Find the computer or server containing the relevant information, search for and view the files to make sure they should be produced, and then copy the files to some type of external media, like a DVD or thumb drive, using the operating system's copy feature. The problem with this approach is that it could potentially lead to spoliation of evidence.

Accessing a file simply to look at it will change the "last accessed" date associated with the file on the source computer. Copying the file will result in the copy having a different date created than the original. If you inadvertently modify the file in the process of reviewing it, the "last modified" date of the source file will also change. Once these timestamp changes are made to the metadata, they cannot be rolled back. Although metadata alteration is not a concern in the vast majority of cases, you must be cognizant of the potential to make inadvertent changes to metadata because, in some cases, it is or could be extremely relevant. Understanding the potential for spoliation and the need to take appropriate precautions in your collection efforts will help you devise an appropriate collection plan.

You must decide at the outset whether metadata is going to be an issue in the case. If it is definitely not, and you obtain a stipulation to that effect from the other side, then you can use the copy function of the operating system and simply copy the relevant data to an external memory device for subsequent distribution and analysis. Expenses will be kept to a minimum, and it is likely that you will not need an outside consultant to help you or your client in the collection process. If metadata is an issue, or is potentially an issue, then a different approach is needed.

The concern over spoliation during the collection process illustrates the importance of an early meet and confer. You must discuss this issue with opposing counsel even before you begin to access and review your client's computer files unless you take appropriate precautions. Likewise, the client should be cautioned not to access the data until you have addressed the issue and devised a plan. Clients cause much inadvertent spoliation by looking at the data out of simple curiosity when litigation begins. Sometimes they do this even if their lawyer warns them not to. Early intervention with the client warning them of the possible adverse consequences of an unsupervised look at the data is a must.

If metadata is not an issue, you should obtain a written stipulation that metadata need not be preserved. However, do not enter into such a stipulation without understanding what you are potentially giving up. Understand at the outset that once you have made a decision that metadata will not be relevant, and you use collection methods that do not preserve metadata, you cannot later undo the decision. If you are uncertain, then you should use defensible collection procedures that will maintain and preserve the metadata. This may require you to consult with outside experts to help in the acquisition process, and you must use specialized tools to collect the data.

In some cases, the best solution will be to engage a computer forensics expert who can make a forensic image of the computer hard drive containing the data you want copied. A forensic image is a byte-for-byte, exact copy of the original. This approach typically requires specialized knowledge and the use of specialized equipment and software. It can be relatively expensive and, in the vast majority of cases, really is overkill. Forensic acquisitions are more often necessary if you are seeking deleted files. Other defensible collection techniques exist, and you might want to consider consulting with an appropriate e-discovery expert or vendor to obtain advice on how to safely collect the data in a nonforensic fashion. If you are properly informed, then it is even possible for you to initiate collection efforts on your own or guide your client's IT staff in their collection efforts.

There are some easy-to-use collection tools available designed specifically for e-discovery. They are relatively inexpensive and do not necessarily require the use of an outside expert. These tools can be used to copy data in a way that preserves the relevant metadata for both the source and copied versions of the file. At the same time, the collection process itself is validated. Preservation involves preserving the file data, its timestamps (when the file was created, last modified, and last accessed), and any other metadata contained within the file. Validation refers to the ability to certify that the contents of the copy are the same as the contents of the original. This usually is done by calculating hash values for the original and copied files. If the hash values match, then you have validated as accurate the copy of the original.

Hash values are the equivalent of an electronic fingerprint. They are alphanumeric values that are calculated by applying a hash algorithm to a string of text, a file, or the entire contents of a hard drive. Common formats include MD5 and SHA-1 hash values. As long as a particular set of data remains unchanged, the source and copy hash values should be the same. If the values are not the same, then some type of alteration to the copied data has occurred.

SafeCopy 2 and Harvester

Pinpoint Labs offers two widely used products to help users obtain defensible collections of ESI. SafeCopy 2 is the base ESI collection tool, whereas

Harvester is the more robust version. Both SafeCopy 2 and Harvester will preserve metadata and timestamp information during the copying process. They allow you to filter what is copied by file type or extension and by date range. Chain-of-custody documentation is automatically prepared as part of the copying process. Copies are also validated using hash values.

Harvester has additional features that SafeCopy 2 lacks. These include the ability to create and deploy remote collections; key word filtering of MS Outlook PST files, Lotus Notes NSF files, loose files, attachments, and archive files; deduplication of multiple PST files; regeneration of PST files; the ability to export e-mail files to eight different message formats; the ability to de-NIST system files; and the ability to filter by file header signature. Work orders can be preconfigured, and jobs can be remotely launched and monitored.

At the time this book was written, SafeCopy 2 and Harvester were available in a variety of different licensing options. Table 5.1 identifies the version, the licensing option, and the current cost for the software.

To understand how the file copying process works using these tools, imagine that you have just been brought into litigation involving the

Table 5.1

PRODUCT	LICENSING OPTIONS	PRICING
SafeCopy 2 Desktop	Licensed to an individual computer.	$161.25
SafeCopy 2 Nomad	Portable license that runs from a flash drive or hard drive. *Nomad* can be easily transferred between devices in different locations.	$448.75
SafeCopy 2 Server	Runs from a central location allowing any computer with access to launch and run a job on the host computer.	$1,311.25 (Three Users)
Harvester Portable	Portable license that runs from a flash drive or hard drive. *Portable* can be transferred between devices in different locations.	$1,495.00
Harvester Server	Runs from a central location allowing any computer with access to launch and run a job on the host computer. Jobs can be remotely launched through the scripting interface, e-mail link, or *Net Harvester*.	$5,598.00 (Three Users)
Harvester Enterprise	Often includes a combination of *Harvester Server* and *Portable* licenses for larger installs that include dozens or hundreds of servers and client licenses.	VARIES
Harvester Collection Kit	Provides a single-use collection license. Complete kits including hard drives and preconfigured job tickets are optional.	$350.00
Net Harvester	Allows users to remotely launch and track *Harvester* jobs from a central location. Jobs are flagged and color coded based on job status. *Net Harvester* maintains a custodian list and can automatically link jobs to sources.	Starts at $3,500.00

use of inside information by a competitor. You determine at your initial client conference that your client has potentially relevant ESI for multiple custodians on a network file server. The custodians also actively save files to the local drives of their individual PCs on an unsupervised basis. They use e-mail extensively, and the e-mail files are maintained on a separate e-mail server. There are several employees whose activities are suspect.

You must quickly develop a plan so you can discuss the issues of preservation and collection at an upcoming meet and confer. The amount of money at stake is relatively modest, and you do not want to break the bank with e-discovery costs. In fact, you would like to rely on internal client resources as much as possible. You are certain you can convince the other side that this is not a case where a computer forensics expert is needed, and you do not want to incur the expense of performing full forensic imaging of every PC and server. At the same time, you know that a forensically defensible collection method should be used in harvesting the ESI, and you want the collection method used to preserve metadata, provide chain-of-custody documentation, and ensure appropriate verification using hash values.

You talk to your favorite e-discovery consultant who tells you that Pinpoint Labs' SafeCopy 2 and Harvester are software products that will handle your identified collection needs. In fact, with appropriate consultation with your client's IT department, your consultant assures you that you can do the collection work yourself. Internal resources can be used to minimize the cost of collection.

In the above hypothetical, it would make sense to do the collection in a phased fashion to determine what really must be collected and preserved. A reasonable plan would be to first check the PCs of the suspect employees involved who are known to save files to their local hard drives. In this case, we want to search for documents, spreadsheets, and design drawings rendered with AutoCad to see if they are storing information locally that should really reside on the company server. If inculpatory information relevant to the potential litigation is found on the PCs, it might make sense to disclose it and engage in immediate settlement negotiations. It would also guide what further e-discovery efforts would be warranted. If no information is found on the local PCs, then a broader search must be made, but the scope and method of the search will be tailored to a search of the file server and the e-mail server. SafeCopy 2 would be a good option for this initial effort.

To begin the process, SafeCopy 2 is loaded onto a USB device. You can then move the device from computer to computer without the need to install the software on the source computer. Paired with a USB external hard drive to use as the target source for the copied files, you have all the tools you need to safely copy information without the fear of altering metadata on the source computer.

Once attached to the computer, the program is launched from the thumb drive. A simple interface that is very intuitive to use opens to create a job ticket. Click on the "Add Source" button for either folders or individual files, browse to the folders or files you want to copy, then click on the "Add Files" button, and you are all set specifying what you want to collect. Next, select the job target path by browsing to the drive where you intend to store the files. This typically would be an external drive you brought along to store the copied ESI.

In this case, we decided to look only at documents, spreadsheets, and AutoCAD files. Using SafeCopy 2, we can input the file extensions of the types of data we want to collect to filter down the number of files copied. We can also insert a date range for the items to be copied. Once these parameters are set, simply click on "Run," and the copying process will begin. A copy of the setup screen for our hypothetical is set forth in Figure 5.1.

Figure 5.1

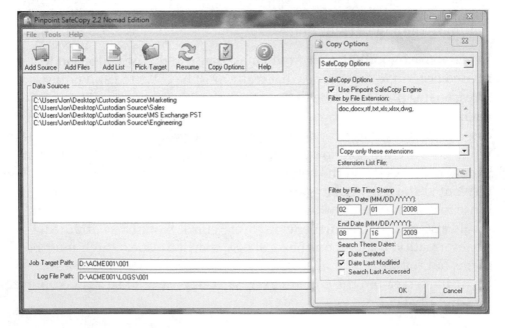

During the copying process, a log file will be generated that identifies a list of each copied file. In addition, it will contain verification information indicating that the hash values of the copied files match the hash values of the source files. The log is generated in CSV format, which can be imported into Excel for easy viewing. A sample of a log file is set forth in Figure 5.2.

Figure 5.2

Source Modified Date	Source Access Date	Source Size	Source MD5	Dest Path
3/24/2009 8:14	3/6/2010 12:43	25290	4F0C58D4996199B4329799E31434370B	G:\ACME Legal Hold\JON-PC\Jon\16-Dec-10\Custodian Source\Fi
8/20/2006 18:34	3/6/2010 12:43	2606	7AF1C660632E9F9456E8776276B53C79	G:\ACME Legal Hold\JON-PC\Jon\16-Dec-10\Custodian Source\Fi
8/20/2006 18:34	8/6/2010 12:43	61082	337744B9596LFEU21082F8008446ED7A	G:\ACME Legal Hold\JON-PC\Jon\16-Dec-10\Custodian Source\Fi
8/20/2006 18:35	3/6/2010 12:43	42574	9285D5CCC27EE26B3D13094BA425C64F	G:\ACME Legal Hold\JON-PC\Jon\16-Dec-10\Custodian Source\Fi
8/20/2006 18:35	3/6/2010 12:43	49324	11EAB7C52C87621AF4CAAF7FCD4D46AB	G:\ACME Legal Hold\JON-PC\Jon\16-Dec-10\Custodian Source\Fi
3/12/2010 18:31	9/21/2010 15:39	36972	A4D175408F6FAF3E6DA7F9CC04D9CA5F	G:\ACME Legal Hold\JON-PC\Jon\16-Dec-10\Custodian Source\W
8/17/2009 10:44	3/6/2010 12:45	2116804	F8629BEE45AB057E744B908DD758C89A	G:\ACME Legal Hold\JON-PC\Jon\16-Dec-10\Custodian Source\W
3/18/2010 22:26	9/21/2010 15:39	11838	7E8859D634D8F4B1F52D274AFD2E902A	G:\ACME Legal Hold\JON-PC\Jon\16-Dec-10\Custodian Source\W
8/20/2006 18:34	3/6/2010 12:43	2606	7AF1C660632E9F9456E8776276B53C79	G:\ACME Legal Hold\JON-PC\Jon\16-Dec-10\Custodian Source\W
8/20/2006 18:34	3/6/2010 12:43	61082	537744B9596CFED21082F8008446ED7A	G:\ACME Legal Hold\JON-PC\Jon\16-Dec-10\Custodian Source\W
8/20/2006 12:30	3/6/2010 12:43	130562	22E1EACFE12CF6C03F40A0C6B14E638D	G:\ACME Legal Hold\JON-PC\Jon\16-Dec-10\Custodian Source\S
8/20/2006 18:30	5/13/2010 13:17	311524	7F716F514A4412212D5C64C703BA1D94	G:\ACME Legal Hold\JON-PC\Jon\16-Dec-10\Custodian Source\S
8/20/2006 18:30	5/13/2010 13:18	189352	6467C9C05BAFF26B9A39CCFEB93C062F	G:\ACME Legal Hold\JON-PC\Jon\16-Dec-10\Custodian Source\S
8/20/2006 18:30	3/6/2010 12:43	189352	6467C9C05BAFF26B9A39CCFEB93C062F	G:\ACME Legal Hold\JON-PC\Jon\16-Dec-10\Custodian Source\S

Assuming for purposes of our hypothetical that we found potentially inculpatory materials on the PCs of two employees, we determine that further investigative efforts are necessary. We want to check the file shares for the suspect custodians on the file server and review their e-mail on the Exchange Server to determine if they have been inappropriately exchanging e-mail with someone outside the company. To do this work, we will use Harvester instead of SafeCopy 2.

In this case, because we intend to collect information from two different servers, we will utilize two different 1 TB external hard drives and install the program directly on each hard drive. Our intention is to set up job tickets on the hard drives and then provide them to the client's IT department to run the actual collection. We will set up two separate collection processes: the first to collect documents, spreadsheets, and AutoCAD files from the file server, and the second to collect the suspect custodians' e-mail from the e-mail server. The two external hard drives will be delivered to the client with instructions to simply connect one external hard drive at a time to the appropriate server using a USB cable.

To set up the hard drives for copying, the program is first downloaded to the external hard drive. Next, after opening the program on the external drive, the collection process is started by creating a job ticket. Using the Job Manager, the person setting up the collection process fills in a number of fields of information. The Job Name is identified, and an Instructions field is available to contain specific collection instructions that will later show up on the job list used by the end user to launch the copy process. An Error Notes field is also available to provide contact information for help if the end user encounters problems running the specific job.

Next, the Sources field is completed. This field contains the file path information for the information to be copied. The selection tool allows you to manually specify a path or a particular folder or file, or import a file list that is a text file containing predefined instructions. The use of a file list is a time saver when the same type of information is sought from multiple computers, and it helps ensure consistency. Typically, you would work with your client's IT department to obtain the necessary pathing information to complete this field.

Next, fill in the Job Target Path by selecting a folder to hold the files that are collected. A similar selection is made for a Log Path for the log report. The copied files and log will be copied to the external hard drive that will be attached to the server via a USB connection.

Harvester next allows you to specify the type of files to copy. This can be done in one of three ways. You can use the selection tool to select file types by category (e.g., e-mail files, office documents, accounting files, etc.), which will copy all file types in that generic category, or you can drill down to the next level by specifying individual file types in the category (e.g., Outlook for e-mail files or Microsoft Office 2007 files for office documents). Alternatively, you can use an extension file list to determine what is copied by importing a text file containing specified file extensions. This allows you to collect, for example, only DOC, DOCX, XLS, and XLSX files.

The copying parameters are set by completing the Action field, which allows you to either include or exclude files by selecting file extensions and by setting a date range to be applied to either the date created, date modified, or date last accessed. This completes the basic information for a job ticket to copy files from the file server. An example of the completed job ticket for the above hypothetical is set forth in Figure 5.3.

A similar process is followed to copy the e-mail files from the Exchange Server. The differences in the job ticket are that the user would click "Advanced" and select the e-mail options. By specifying "Search Outlook Accounts," Exchange e-mail accessible to the default account can be searched and collected into a PST file. Several additional options that can be selected include specifying e-mail accounts/domains, key words, date ranges, removing duplicates and regenerating new PSTs, or exporting to eight different message formats.

Figure 5.3

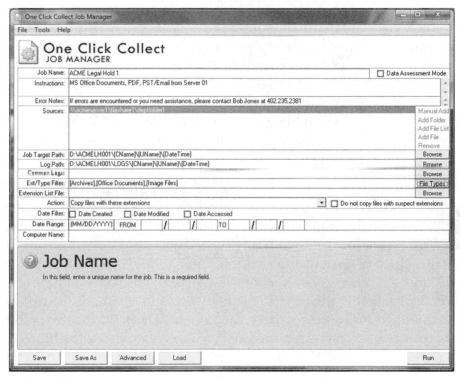

A sample job ticket for e-mail collection is set forth in Figure 5.4.

Figure 5.4

There are further advanced options in Harvester that allow you to create full paths, copy empty folders, exclude temp files, exclude system files, hash the source and destination files, and make a variety of other selection options that may be of use depending on the situation. Other useful advanced features available only in the Harvester version are the ability to apply a de-NISTing filter and to run in silent mode so that the individual whose PC is copied is never aware the process is occurring. Another advanced feature is the ability to create scripts that can be used to create job files, start a job, and launch programs or utilities that can work with the data capture and the files collected.

Once the job ticket is complete and the collection drive is attached to the servers from which the data is to be harvested, Harvester is then run, and the files are automatically copied to the specified folder on the external hard drive. A log file is automatically created and stored. This CSV file contains chain-of-custody information. Later, it can be imported into Excel, and you can generate a report that specifies the date and time a file was copied; whether the hashes matched; the source path; the source created, modified, and accessed dates; the source MD5 Hash; the destination path; the destination created, modified, and accessed dates; the file size; and the destination MD5 Hash.

Another more advanced feature to be aware of is that with Harvester you can easily activate and deactivate the license. This means that once a job has been run using the program installed on the first collection drive, it can easily be deactivated, and the program installation on the second external drive can be activated. This is particularly useful if you are collecting data from different parts of the country. If you sent a drive to Los Angeles and another to New York, as soon as the collection in Los Angeles was done and the software was deactivated, the software on the New York drive could be activated and the collection run. This feature avoids the need to purchase multiple licenses of Harvester. You can even e-mail the program and the job tickets to an IT person at the collection site. They would copy the program and job tickets to an external hard drive and run the process themselves.

The above examples show that it is possible for a lawyer who understands the process to engage in self-collection methods using the appropriate tools. You might ultimately feel more comfortable enlisting the aid of an e-discovery expert or vendor to help you with your collection efforts. However, working directly with technical support from Pinpoint Labs, you could supervise the collection activities of your client's ESI in a defensible way. It is even possible for you to use similar techniques to collect ESI from the opposing side if they are willing to cooperate and you are willing to share the results with them. Thus, relatively inexpensive tools can be used for self-collection efforts that produce reliable copies of ESI.

The key to collection in small cases is to understand what you need at the outset and to devise a plan to collect it in a defensible manner. If metadata is not an issue, the process can be simple and inexpensive. If metadata is potentially a concern, then more elaborate steps must be taken. However, it is possible to use self-collection methods to preserve metadata on the source computer and ensure that the copies of the files have the same metadata as the original files. Even where metadata is an issue, it makes sense to work with the other side to arrive at stipulated collection methods. Early meet and confers are a must. Assuming you can arrive at an agreement, a written collection protocol should be developed and included in a stipulation. If you have covered your bases following the above advice and utilizing the techniques described, then you can minimize the cost of obtaining ESI in small cases.

CHAPTER SIX

Quickly Viewing a Mixed Bag of ESI

IT IS NOT UNUSUAL in small cases to receive a CD or DVD with a relatively small number of computer files. Typically, this is a mixed bag of electronic files in multiple formats. You might receive ESI that includes document files; spreadsheet files; PDF, TIFF, and ZIP files; and extracted e-mail files. If you want, you can view each one by opening it in its native application. The problem with this approach is that you must open each file one by one, taking the time to open the specific application and then load the file for each item you wish to view. Not only is the process time consuming, but you may not happen to have all the native applications installed on your computer to view the documents. You can go out and buy and install the software, but is it really necessary to own every program in order to view the files typically found in a CD or DVD of files produced in response to a request for production of documents? The simple answer is "no."

Quick View Plus

Using an inexpensive viewer like Quick View Plus Standard Edition (QVP) (available as a $49 download from **www.Avantstar.com**), you can view files in over 300 formats without the need to own the actual native applications. This includes word processing, spreadsheet, database, presentation, compression, graphic, and other formats. Using QVP you can rapidly navigate through the list of files on your CD or DVD, opening one after the other in quick succession without the need to invoke the native application. Everything you need to view a collection of documents in one program can be done within QVP.

In Figure 6.1, you can see that the QVP desktop is divided into three panes. The viewer is on the right, and on the left you will find the navigation panes that include a tree view of your computer folders on top, and below that a specific list of files contained in the folder you have highlighted up top. Click on any specific file to open in the QVP viewer. On the button bar, you can choose to close the navigation panes to have a full desktop view of the document. You can move from document to document using the arrows on the button bar. You can also open multiple windows to simultaneously view multiple documents. For documents containing text, you can search for a specific word and move from highlighted hit to hit. You can also launch the document for editing in its native application by clicking on the icon in the button bar. Finally, you can print the document by clicking on the "Print" button.

QVP is an inexpensive solution for quickly viewing a collection of miscellaneous files. Avantstar also offers a more advanced version of QVP in its Professional Edition. The Professional Edition costs $570 (and includes the first year of required support and maintenance). Five seats are

Figure 6.1

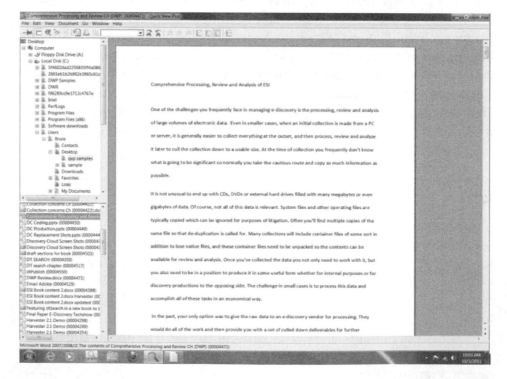

included with the license. The Professional Edition is specifically targeted to the legal market. It has all the features and functionality of the Standard Edition plus additional features.

Perhaps the most significant feature for e-discovery purposes is the fact that you can see everything, including the metadata, in a document you have selected to view. An example showing the metadata and rendered view of a Microsoft Word document is set forth in Figure 6.2.

Figure 6.2

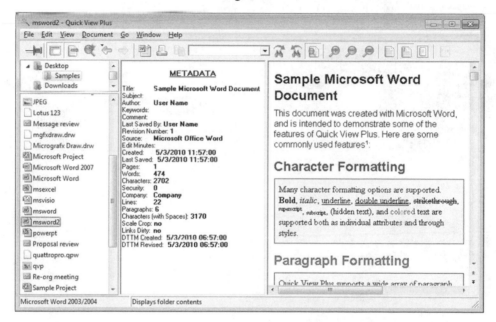

Unlike the Standard Edition, where you can search for key words one document at a time, the Professional Edition has an Auto Search and Highlight function that allows you to navigate multiple documents with a single search. Furthermore, the hits are highlighted in both the text of the document and in the metadata. See Figure 6.3.

You can also copy and paste any portion of a viewed file into another application. Finally, you can bulk print documents without the need to view each one prior to printing. This is a useful feature when you have done a quick sampling of collected documents and know they are the ones you want to print to PDF or paper for production purposes. You can even create a ZIP file within the program to create a production set.

Figure 6.3

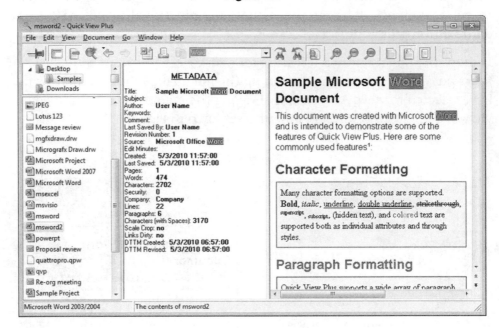

CHAPTER SEVEN

Small Budget
Searching
Solutions

IN SMALL CASES WHERE preservation of metadata concerns do not exist, it is not unusual for parties to a litigation to simply bulk copy multiple computer files that may have some bearing on the case. These files typically will be presented to you on a CD or DVD in the form of raw files in mixed file formats. The files will not be searchable as presented, and you must open each file in its native application in order to view it. A small collection may be limited to several hundred files and, in such cases, you do not really need to employ a full-blown litigation support application. Nevertheless, you need a way to make sense of what you have received with the ability to both search and view the documents in the collection.

dtSearch Desktop

One of the most economical solutions to meet this need is dtSearch Desktop. At a cost of only $199 per license, dtSearch Desktop offers a robust tool for processing, searching, and viewing a mixed collection of raw files and e-mail files. At this price it is ideal for use with small collections. However, do not make the mistake of thinking that because of the modest price dtSearch Desktop cannot be used with much larger collections. It works equally well with collections that are terabytes in size. In fact, dtSearch Desktop is the search engine that is used in many of the popular and more expensive litigation support applications on the market. Those software manufacturers have licensed the dtSearch Desktop technology and, as licensees, do not advertise that they are actually using a third-party application as the underlying search engine. The fact that dtSearch Desktop is widely used in such a fashion is further evidence that it is a tool that can meet your searching needs, whether your collection is a few hundred files, a few thousand files, or many more.

Assume for purposes of our discussion on dealing with e-discovery in small cases that you receive a DVD with 1 GB of miscellaneous computer files. The files of interest include a couple of Microsoft Outlook PST files containing e-mail, multiple Word and WordPerfect documents, some simple text files, some Excel spreadsheets, and multiple PDF files. There are also miscellaneous system files included on the DVD that are really of no concern. You want to take these raw files and create a searchable collection of documents.

To start the process you must copy the data on the DVD to the hard drive of the workstation on which dtSearch Desktop is installed. Next, you must open the dtSearch Desktop program. From there, you must index your collection. This is the most time-consuming process, but it prepares the collection of documents for subsequent use by indexing the location of each word in each file. Once the collection is indexed, searching is nearly instantaneous.

To index the documents, select "Create index" from the Index drop-down menu. This opens a Create index dialog box shown as Figure 7.1 in which you name the database, browse to the location where you want the index stored, and determine whether a summary or detailed list of indexed files is required.

Figure 7.1

After you click "OK," you will be asked if you want to add documents to the index. Click "Yes," then go to the Update Index dialog box, shown as Figure 7.2.

Figure 7.2

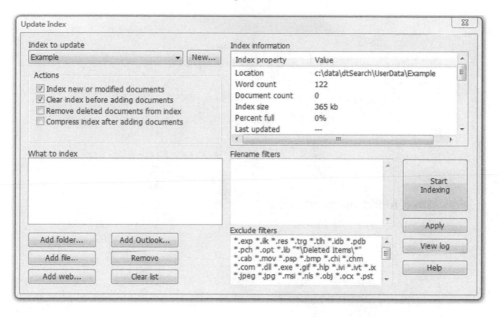

Using this dialog box, you can determine whether to index new or modi-fied documents, clear the existing index before adding documents, remove deleted documents from the index, or compress the index after adding documents. Select the appropriate actions by checking those options you wish to activate. Next, add materials by using the features in the "What to index" portion of the dialog box. Using the available but-tons, you can add folders, add individual files, add information from the Web, and even add folders from Microsoft Outlook to the index. Clicking on the appropriate button will enable you to browse to the location of the items you wish to add to the index. Note that in the "Exclude filters" sec-tion of the dialog box, it is possible to specify by extension those types of files you wish to exclude from the indexing process, such as the miscella-neous system files that were included on the DVD that are not relevant to our hypothetical matter at hand. Once all of the necessary selections are made, click "Start Indexing," and the indexing process will begin. Once the indexing process is complete, every word in the collection is available for searching.

Upon completion of the indexing process, a report can be generated, shown as Figure 7.3, that identifies the date and start/stop times the indexing process was run, the total number of words in the index, the total number of documents contained in the index, the number of documents indexed, the bytes of indexed data, and the documents that were removed from the index. For documents that were unable

Figure 7.3

Index Update Report

C:\Users\Bruce\AppData\Local\dtSearch\Sample Index	
Actions:	*Create Add Compress RemoveDeleted*
Result:	*OK*
Start	*9/27/2011 10:16:11 AM*
End	*9/27/2011 10:16:33 AM*

Documents indexed

Total words in index	*32,491*
Total documents in index	*1,109*
Documents indexed	*1,109*
Bytes indexed	*231,710 kb*
Documents removed	*0*

Documents not indexed

Documents not indexed	*0*
Encrypted files	*0*
Unreadable files	*0*
Skipped as "binary"	*0*

Documents partially indexed

Partially encrypted files	*0*
Partially unreadable files	*0*

to be indexed, the report identifies the number of documents that did not process and indicates those that were encrypted or unreadable or that were skipped as binary files. Partially indexed files are identified as well. Finally, you can generate a list of the documents that were not indexed if needed.

To begin to search the indexed files, click on the "Search" button on the button bar or select "Search" from the Search drop-down menu to open the Search dialog box, shown as Figure 7.4.

The top right of the dialog box shows a list of the indexes that are available for searching. You can search in one or more than one index at a time. The "Indexed word list" is located at the top left of the dialog box, and it shows a list of all the words that are currently available for search-

Figure 7.4

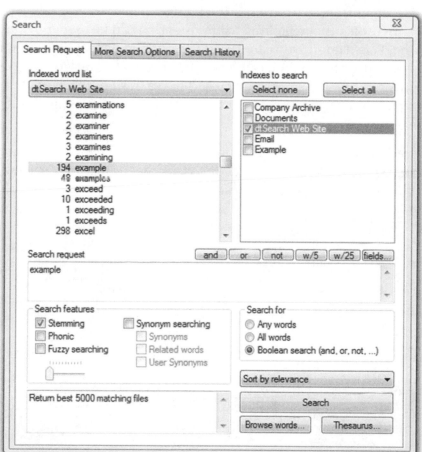

ing in the index. In the example above, the word "example" appears 194 times in the dtSearch Desktop Web site index. You can insert the word "example" into the "Search request" box, and it will return the 194 hits identified in the word list. It is possible to expand the search results on the word "example" if you enable the "Stemming," "Fuzzy searching," or "Synonym searching" search features. Stemming, for example, would return all incidences of the word "example" and "examples." Depending on the sensitivity you set, fuzzy searching would return additional hits such as "examining" and "examines." It also helps by accommodating typos. Synonym searching would return those documents that have the word "example" in them, along with documents containing synonyms such as "sample" or "exemplar."

Note that to the right, just above the "Search request" box, there are a series of buttons that can be used to build a Boolean string search if you want to construct a more advanced search. These buttons allow you to use the "and, or, not, and within a specified range" commands to refine your search. There are other searching techniques that can be used in Boolean searching. For example, you can use quotation marks around phrases to search for entire phrases. You can insert "+" in front of any word or phrase to require it in the search results, or insert "-" in front of the word or phrase to exclude it. Other more advanced searching techniques are also available.

In Figure 7.5, under the "Search Request" tab, a search request was run on the word "eDiscovery" in the Testdb database. Stemming was selected, and a limitation of the best 5,000 matches was set.

Figure 7.5

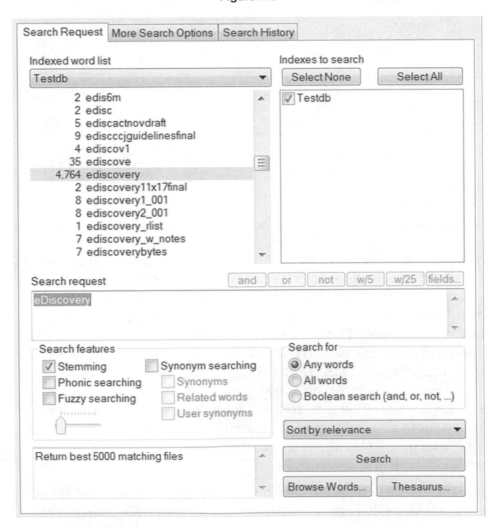

To further refine the search, the "More Search Options" tab was selected, shown in Figure 7.6. In addition to setting the search results options to return a maximum of 5,000 files and to stop searching after 25,000 files, the "File modification date" drop-down menu is highlighted in Figure 7.6 to show how you can select a date range based on the last modified date. Additional search options are also demonstrated.

Figure 7.6

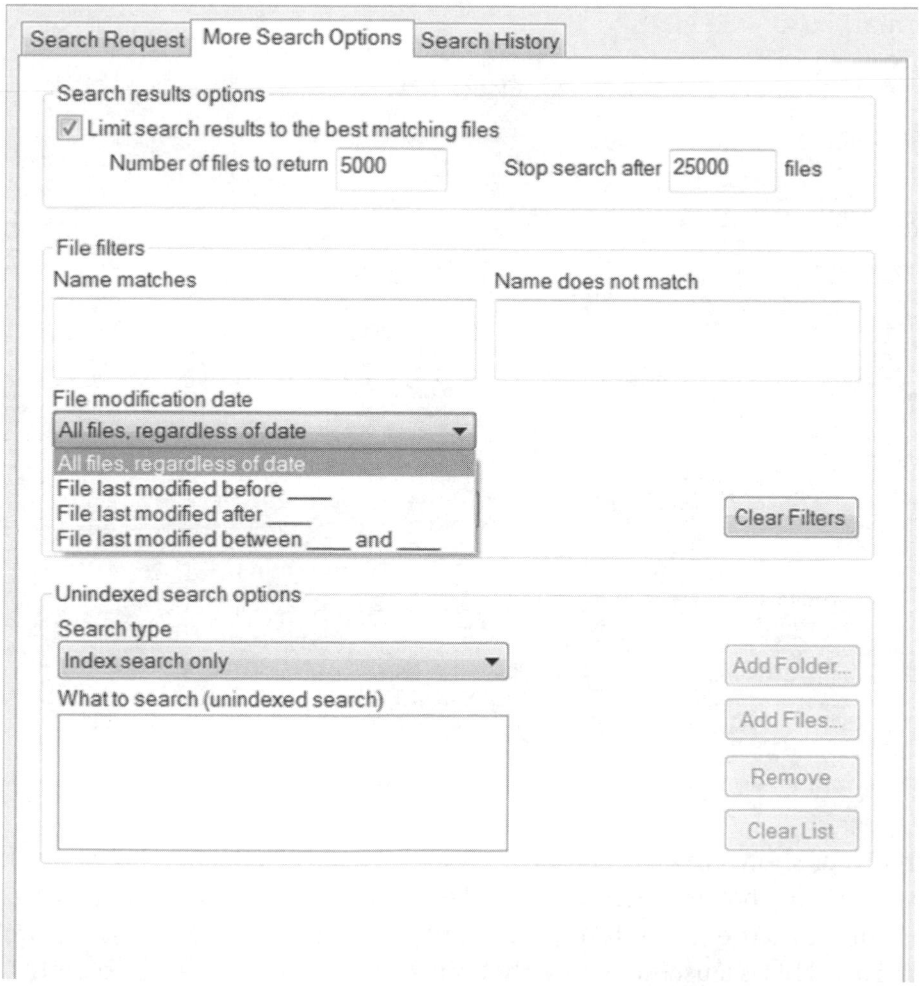

The search results screen in the form of a spreadsheet report is set forth in Figure 7.7. Retrieved documents will sort by relevance as the default; however, you can sort by date or search by number of hits in each document by clicking the column headers to change the sort order. Additional information regarding each document is set forth in the spreadsheet. If desired, a report of the spreadsheet results can be saved or printed.

In Figure 7.7, a split screen is shown with the top-half of the spreadsheet containing the search results and the bottom-half containing a rendering of the highlighted document that was selected. The search term is highlighted in yellow. There are right and left arrow buttons on the button bar that allow you to move forward or backward from hit to hit. Buttons also exist to help you navigate from document to document. If you wish, you can select the button on the button bar containing the pencil and note, or hit "F8" on your keyboard, and the selected item will open in its native format.

Figure 7.7

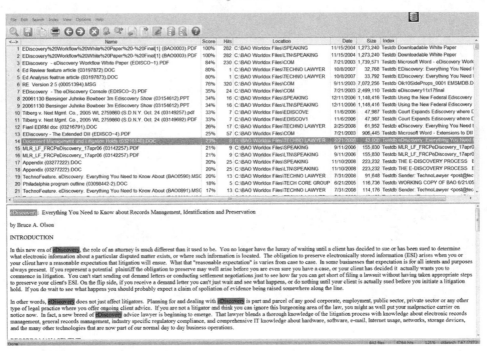

Finally, as shown in Figure 7.8, the "Search History" tab is available on the Search dialog box to generate a list of each search that was run. The history provides the search term, the number of hits, and the date the search was run. This is a useful feature that allows you to repeat a prior search and generate the same search results by simply selecting and double clicking on the desired search term or by highlighting a search and then clicking the "Open" button.

Figure 7.8

All of the common file formats you are likely to encounter are searchable using dtSearch Desktop. It is a logical solution to managing smaller amounts of ESI commonly received in small cases. It enables you to search and view everything in the collection without the need to purchase more expensive litigation support alternatives. Its use is not limited to small cases, but for those who typically deal with small cases, dtSearch Desktop is an affordable and robust solution.

CHAPTER EIGHT

A Processing, Review, and Production Tool All in One

AS E-DISCOVERY BECOMES A normal part of every litigated matter, including small- to mid-sized cases where the potential cost of e-discovery can rival the value of the litigated claim, the need for an economical way to process, analyze, review, and produce the relevant ESI is critical. The terms "e-discovery" and "bargain" rarely are found together in the same sentence. However, in the case of Digital WarRoom Pro (DWR Pro), they really do belong together. At a cost of only $895 for a single-seat installation when this book was written, DWR Pro offers a feature-rich, PC-based, e-discovery application for rapid processing, review, and production of small- to medium-sized document collections (typically in the range of 500,000 documents or less). Multiuser, network-based solutions are also available for additional cost, and the program can be deployed just as successfully against much larger collections in a team environment.

Digital WarRoom Pro

DWR Pro offers an end-to-end solution to deal with ESI from identification through processing, analysis, review, and production. Collected custodian ESI, including PST and ZIP files as well as native files, can be quickly processed for review. This includes the option of de-NISTing to remove application software, .EXE files, and other files not relevant to e-discovery. Container files and e-mail files are automatically extracted during processing. The entire collection is then indexed and hashed, and a document database is created for analysis, review, and production purposes.

Early case assessment tools and sophisticated search filters are available to help you identify key topics and relationships at the outset of your work. Once the data is processed, you can review the document collection and slice and dice it in a myriad of ways to determine and mark what should be produced. Thereafter, production sets in either native or image format are easy to create. They can be redacted as needed and automatically stamped with production numbers and other key markings and endorsements. Finally, an extensive series of built-in reports allows you to assess and manage your collection during each phase of the process from intake through production.

Installation requires a two-step process, and you must understand up front that some additional software is required for DWR Pro to function properly. First, you need an installation of Microsoft Office Professional 2007 or later on the PC on which you install DWR Pro. You also need Internet Explorer 6.0 SP1 set as the default browser and Microsoft .NET Framework 4.0 or later. The program will run on Windows XP Professional SP2, but Windows 7 Professional with 4 GB RAM and at least 160 GB of hard drive space is recommended. You must also purchase and install Quick View Plus to serve as a viewer ($49). You must first install SQL Server Express (at no additional cost) prior to installing DWR Pro, but once that is done, the balance of the program installation is simple and straightforward.

A typical Windows application interface is used. If you are familiar with Microsoft Outlook, you will easily be able to navigate the program menus and controls in the frames on the left side of your screen. As set forth in Figure 8.1, the document "Review" window in the main workspace provides a document list in grid format similar to Microsoft Excel.

Figure 8.1

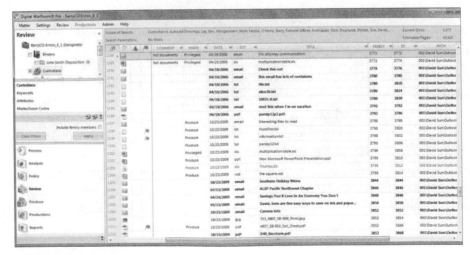

The document browser pane (Figure 8.2), where a selected document is reviewed, can be positioned in any quadrant of the main screen, the same screen, or dragged onto a second monitor allowing you to use dual monitors for an expanded view.

Figure 8.2

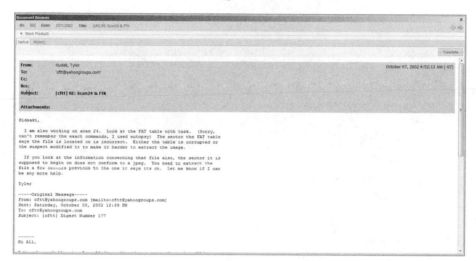

Adding data to the program is simple. Activate the "Process Documents" menu to either browse through the explorer tree to the collections of processed data, or drag and drop new folders of custodian data onto the processing window (Figure 8.3). Each folder of data is profiled using the date of acquisition, the name of the collection, the name of the person who acquired the data, the client, and any relevant notes as descriptors.

Figure 8.3

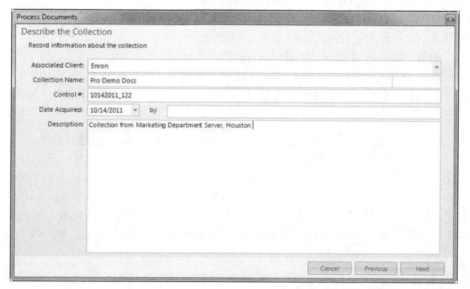

You have the option at this point of extracting ZIP files, PST files, and other container files automatically. You can also remove operating system and application files using a de-NIST process. The "Admin" tab provides a link to download the current NSRL library from the DWR Pro Web site. See Figure 8.4.

Figure 8.4

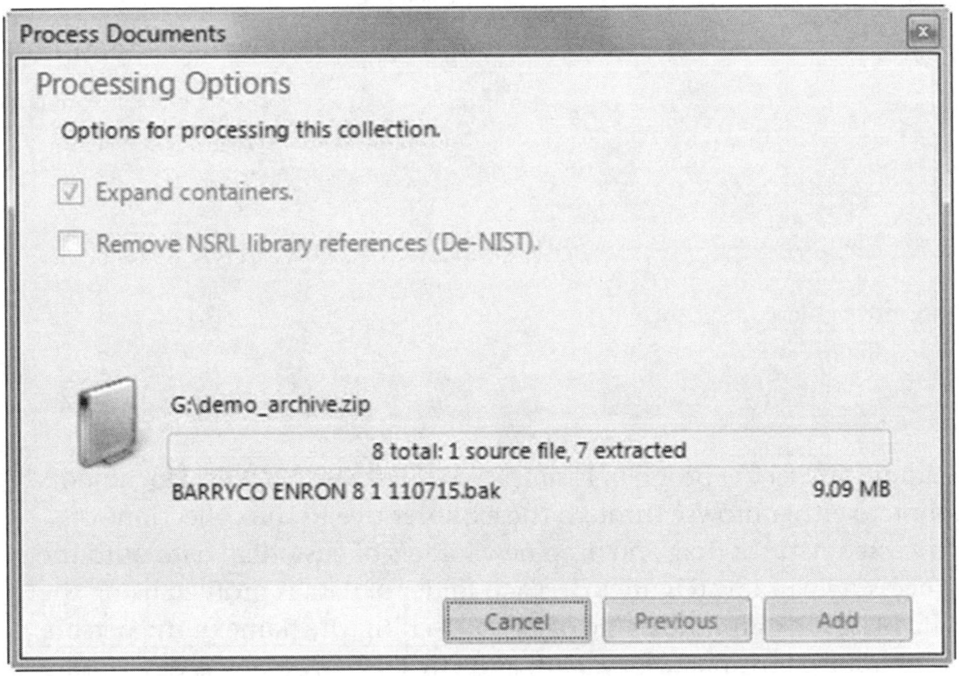

When adding ESI collections from custodians, you have the ability to import the data and associated load files to automatically code fields of information in the database. An exception report showing any items that were password protected, corrupt, or failed to process properly is automatically generated. A collections report and processing history log are also created and automatically updated as new items are added to the collection.

As shown in Figure 8.5, policies can be applied that allow deduping within custodian or across the matter, or to retain duplicate documents. Date-range limitations and file-type limitations are available to provide early culling. For example, you can set the parameters to process content created on or after June 1, 2008, that include documents, spreadsheets, and e-mail. The balance of the files in the raw data will not be processed.

Figure 8.5

Once the data collections are loaded and indexed, a number of early case assessment tools are available to help you quickly determine the size and composition of the case database. As shown in Figure 8.6, a "What If" report can be analyzed in grid view using a variety of comparative factors, including custodian, collection, file extension, and key word. For exam-

Figure 8.6

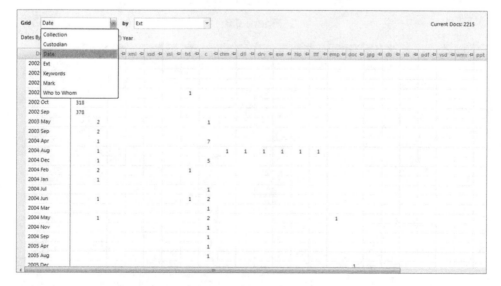

ple, you can generate a report that shows each category of data by extension type for each individual collection of documents in the total collection to quickly determine where the bulk of the case data resides and what type of file types are involved. This helps you determine the number of files you must review to help develop a review budget.

As shown in Figure 8.7, a "Who to Whom" analysis of e-mail is another early case assessment tool that provides a graphical view of the number of e-mail contacts one individual had with another individual. This allows you to determine early on whose e-mail should be reviewed initially.

Figure 8.7

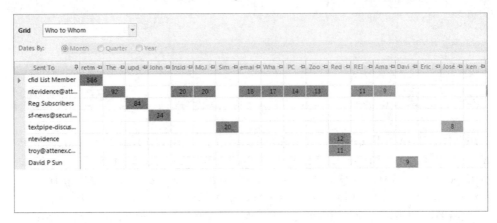

Once you have loaded the data and indexed it, the full collection is available for review (see Figure 8.8). The spreadsheet view of the collection can

Figure 8.8

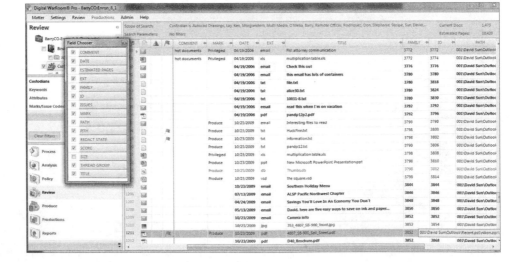

be sorted by column, the columns can be dragged and dropped to a new position or dragged off the screen, and you can select which columns to view from a pick list.

As shown in Figure 8.9, the amount of information visible in the spreadsheet can be further filtered by file extensions, custodians, key words, or other more advanced filters that use Boolean search terms to create more complex search parameters.

Figure 8.9

In the review process, you can mark items for privilege, responsiveness, and production, as well as issue code them. Coding can be done on a per-document basis using a work product palette containing the check box "Marks/Issue Codes." See Figure 8.10.

Figure 8.10

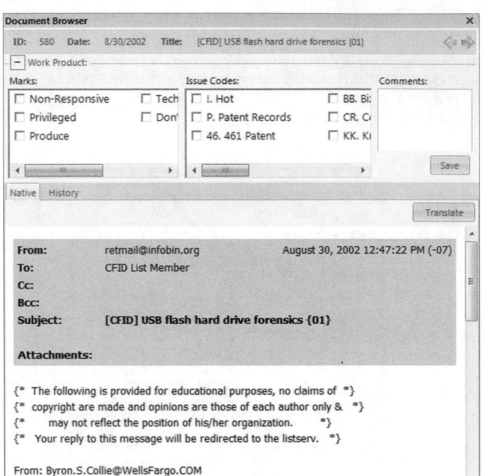

In the Settings menu, you can create user-defined issue codes specific to the case. See Figure 8.11.

You can also right click on an item to obtain standard marking options when working in the spreadsheet view. As shown in Figure 8.12, you can select multiple items in the spreadsheet view and bulk mark them as well.

The viewer will provide a rendered view of each document you select as it appears in its native format, as set forth in Figure 8.13.

Figure 8.11

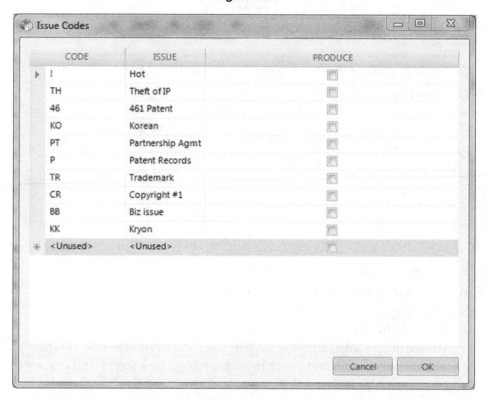

Figure 8.12

Figure 8.13

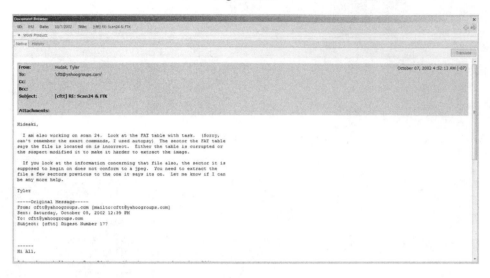

Foreign language content based on the Roman alphabet, Cyrillic, and Asian language character sets can be processed, indexed, and searched within DWR Pro. The Document Browser contains a translation option that will automatically translate non-English content and display the translation, assisting the reviewer in identifying the subject and content of the document. See Figure 8.14.

Figure 8.14

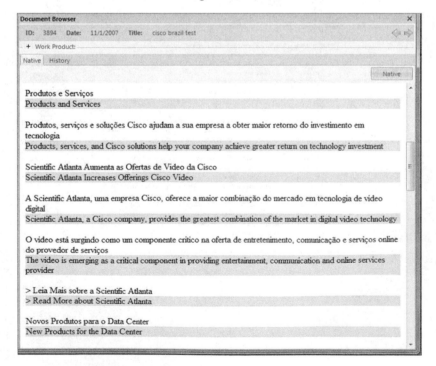

As shown in Figure 8.15, a "History" tab is available in the Document Browser window that contains a summary report of all marks and tags for a given item, allowing a higher-level reviewer to easily make appropriate adjustments to the item's status prior to production.

Figure 8.15

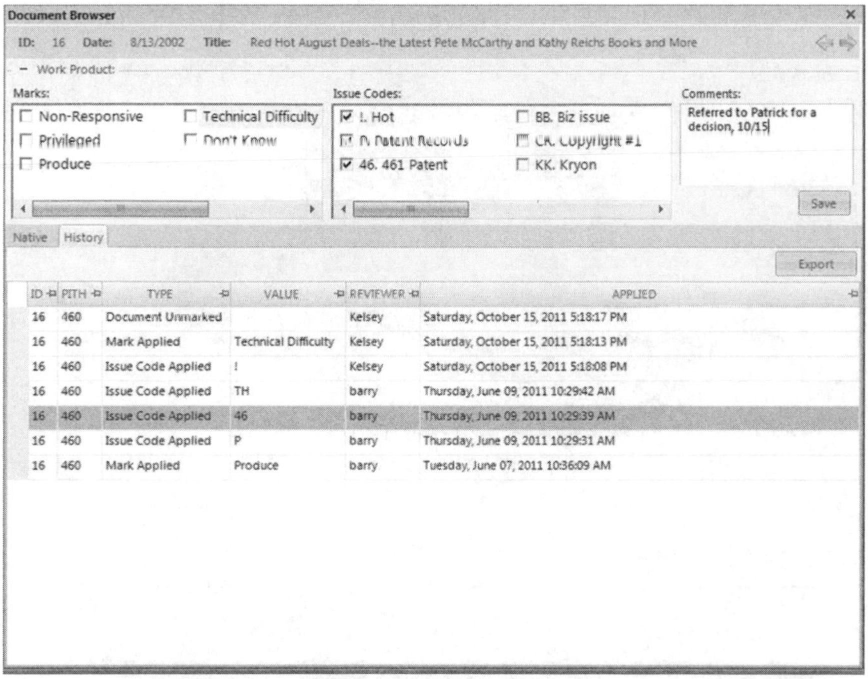

E-mail can be searched and filtered using a sender/recipient option or by the domain name of the sender or receiver. See Figure 8.16. E-mail search by the use of key words in the e-mail header is also supported.

Figure 8.16

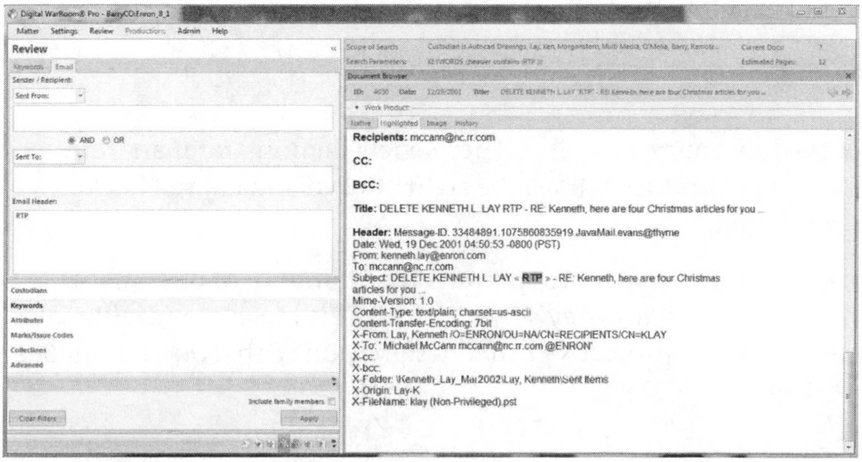

As the collection is reviewed, items that are potentially subject to document production can be flagged on an ongoing basis. They can subsequently be further reviewed as a subset of the total collection, and determinations can be made for purposes of redaction. Redactions appear as shown in Figure 8.17.

Figure 8.17

As set forth in Figure 8.18, if further review demonstrates an item should not be produced, it can be right clicked and clawed back from the production.

Right-click functionality also permits the stamping of documents with "Confidential" or "Attorney's Eyes Only." This is a customizable selection to associate a protective order designation with a document. See Figure 8.19.

Figure 8.18

BEG BATE	END BATES	EXT	ID	PHASE	TYPE	MARK	STATE	PAGES	PITH
1	1	email	3962	Produce	Image	Produce	Released	1	463
2	2	email	3964	Produce	Image	Produce	Released	1	740
3	3	email	3978	Produce	Image	Produce	Released	1	713
4	4	email	3976	Produce	Image	Produce	Released	1	1010
5	5	email	3992	Produce	Image		Released	1	1196
6	6	email		Add to depo binder... ▶	age	Produce	Clawback	1	1089
7	7	email		Add to other binder... ▶	age	Produce	Clawback	1	908
8	8	email			age	Produce	Released	1	960
9	9	email		Clawback	age	Produce	Released	1	953
10	10	email		Comments...	age	Produce	Released	1	353
11	11	email		Copy value	age	Produce	Released	2	293
13	13	email	4028	Produce	Image	Produce	Released	1	360
14	20	email	4026	Produce	Image	Produce	Released	7	521

Figure 8.19

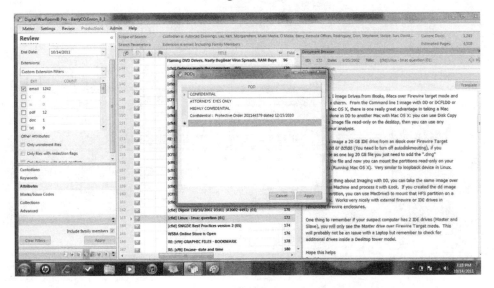

Other endorsements can be added as needed. As set forth in Figure 8.20, a graphical layout tool helps you design the final production format.

Once the production set has been triaged and finalized, it can be exported as either a native or a TIFF image production set. The production set can then be copied to CD/DVD or placed on a thumb drive or external hard drive for delivery to the opposing side.

During the review phase, the use of subfolders called "binders" is supported. This allows you to create multiple, unique sets of documents for use as discovery productions, for depositions, for distribution to a particular expert, or for trial exhibits. See Figure 8.21.

Figure 8.20

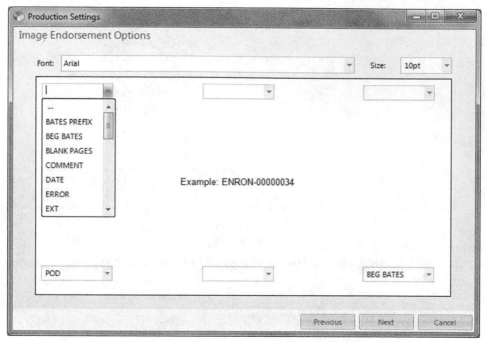

Figure 8.21

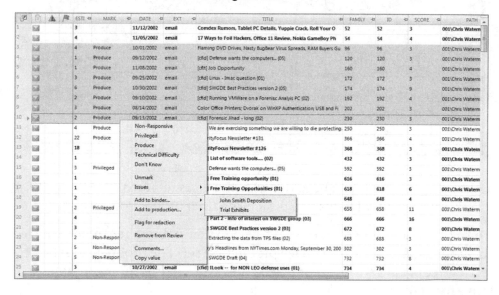

As shown in Figure 8.22, a binder can be produced and exported to external media with a right-click "Export Binder" command or from binder properties.

One of the most important features of DWR Pro is its extensive reporting capability. The many built-in report options provide a detailed under-

Figure 8.22

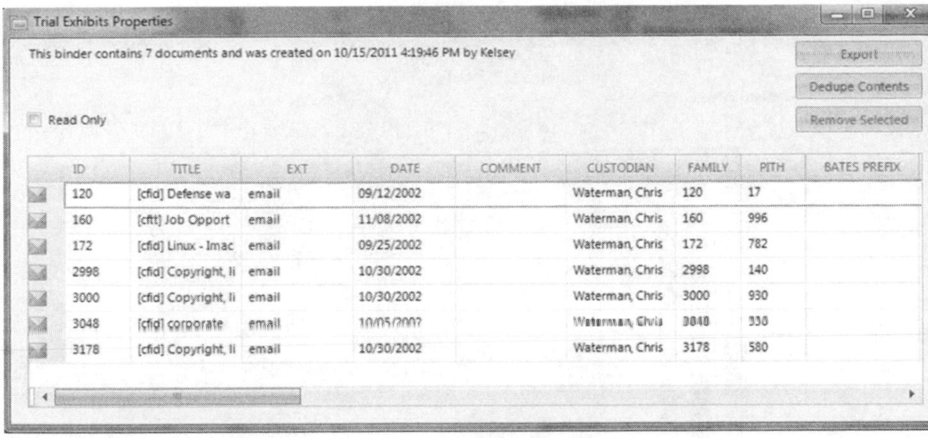

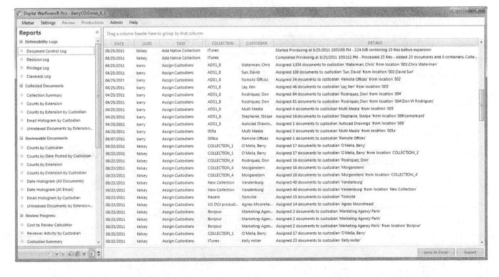

standing of the collection and offer enhanced management as the case is developed over time. A number of different categories and types of reports can be generated, including useful histograms for visual assessment of case data.

Defensibility logs, including reports for document control, privilege, and clawback, can be created. See Figure 8.23.

Figure 8.23

The collection as a whole can be analyzed in reports by document summary, extension, extension by custodian, and more. A particularly helpful report in this category is the histogram of e-mail by custodian, as set forth in Figure 8.24. This visual timeline of e-mail by date may help identify collection gaps.

Figure 8.24

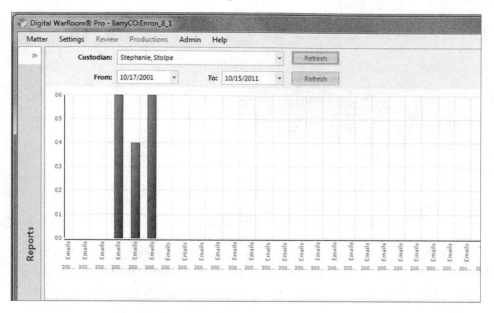

The progress of the review can even be managed using reports that include a cost-to-review calculator, a reviewer activity log, and an assignment progress log. See Figure 8.25.

Figure 8.25

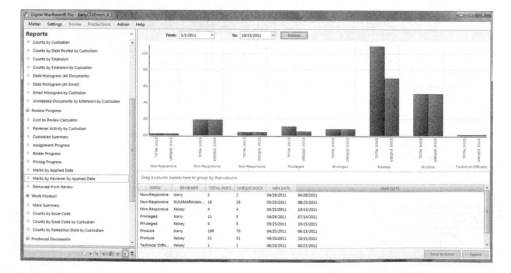

Marks and tags that are made during review are summarized in a report, as shown in Figure 8.26.

Figure 8.26

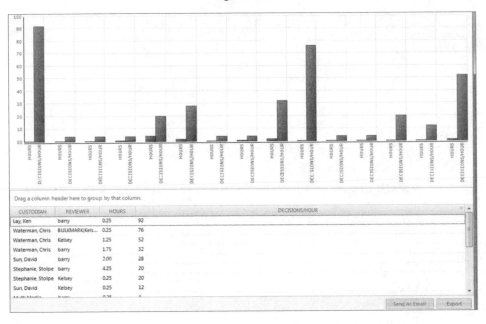

Production reports can be created, including a production summary, a summary by custodian, a summary by extension, and a Bates gap analysis that is useful in making sure productions are properly Bates stamped in appropriate sequence. See Figure 8.27.

Figure 8.27

PDS	RANGE	STATE	GAP REPORT
PDS001	ENRON-00000001 to ENRON-00000033 (33 pages)	Finalized	Bates gap detected between 5 and 8 Bates gap detected between 31 and 33
PDS002	ENRON-00000034 to ENRON-00000246 (213 pages)	Draft	Bates gap detected between 36 and 69
US DOJ production 1	ENRON00000634 to ENRON00000662 (29 pages)	Finalized	Bates gap detected between 636 and 639
PDS007	ENRON-00000034 to ENRON-00000075 (42 pages)	Draft	No Bates gaps detected.
PDS008	ENRON-00000034 to ENRON-00000037 (4 pages)	Draft	No Bates gaps detected.
PDS009	ENRON-00000034 to ENRON-00000064 (31 pages)	Draft	No Bates gaps detected.

Portable Archive File

If the case grows beyond the size that a single user with DWR Pro can complete, the case transfers easily to the WorkGroup server version for multiuser teams or to DWR Pro's hosted platform. The archive file used to transfer information contains all case data plus document marks, annotations, and all other work product. Similarly, an archive file produced from a hosted or server-based matter may be stored for in-house reference and opened in DWR Pro. See Figure 8.28.

Figure 8.28

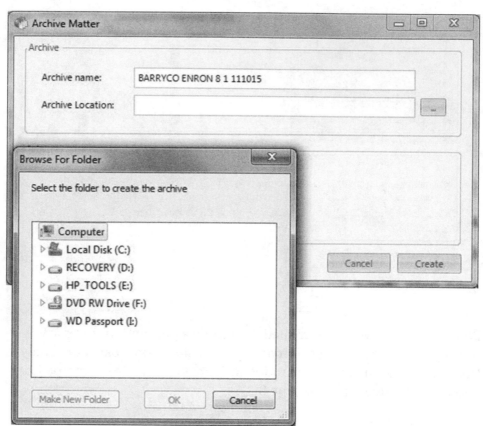

DWR Pro is an economical yet full-featured tool that can help you manage the multiple stages of the e-discovery process. It is an ideal solution for managing smaller collections of documents, although it works just as well on large cases. It can serve as your primary review tool as well as your processing tool, or you can create a load file containing a set of relevant documents to be loaded into any other litigation support or review tool you use.

CHAPTER NINE

Managing Large Volumes of E-Mail and Attachments

BEFORE THE ERA OF e-discovery, a favorite way to confound the opposition was to make a warehouse full of records available for review, handing the key to the lawyer, and saying, "Have at it, you've got 24 hours to complete your review." This was a blatant effort to shift the search burden and expense to the requesting party. Paralegals and lawyers found themselves searching through banker's box after banker's box of documents attempting to locate relevant materials that were often disorganized, miscategorized, or even intentionally hidden in plain sight. They were also under tremendous time pressure to complete their review, which often led to less-than-thorough discovery.

In the electronic world, the equivalent of this abusive practice is the data dump. Opposing parties turn over disks, DVDs, or even external hard drives full of gigabytes of data, all in native format, without an index or a way to intelligently review the materials produced. Because e-mail is such an important component of modern e-discovery, it is also common to receive the contents of multiple custodians' e-mail shares as PST files where each file is several gigabytes in size. When fully processed with attachments extracted, the size of these files can multiply to three to five times or more than the original size of the source file. To review each and every item on a linear basis would simply take too much time, and just as with paper documents in the warehouse, the likelihood is that only a fraction of these materials are actually relevant to the case.

Intella

Intella by Vound Software is a software program that lets you make an early case assessment. You can then process and quickly analyze the electronic data you receive to easily reduce the volume of materials to those that are truly relevant. It offers visualization tools to help you better understand the nature of your collection. You can search e-mail, attachments, archives, headers, and metadata. You can use Intella to group and trace e-mail threads. You can preview, cull, and dedupe your collection. It will also help you produce the relevant items in an electronic format that is ultimately usable in a variety of litigation support applications or in PDF format.

Intella is very simple to install and use. It is designed to operate on computers that are "off the shelf." It supports Windows 2000, 2003, XP, Vista, and Windows 7. The minimum hardware configuration is an Intel Pentium 4 CPU, 2 GHz with 2 GB RAM. An Intel Core Duo CPU with 4 GB RAM is recommended. After installation of the software, you must use the dongle provided to access the data because Vound protects its software with the HASP SRM software.

When you start the program, you have the option of opening an existing case or starting a new case in the Intella Case Manager. As shown in Figure 9.1, a new case will contain the case name, a description of the case,

Figure 9.1

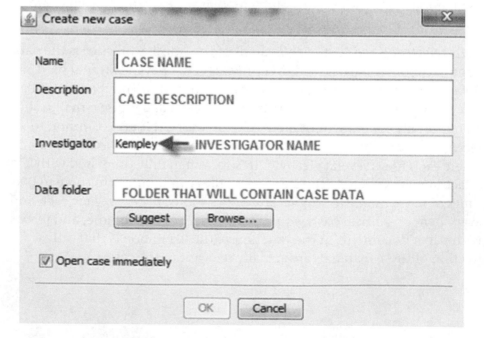

the name of the primary investigator, and the data folder where the case contents are stored.

Source data is added using the "Add New Source" wizard, as set forth in Figure 9.2. You have the option of loading a folder of materials or individual PST, OST, DBX, NSF, or Mbox files and IMAP accounts. The folder option is used if you have multiple PST or other e-mail files or a mixed collection of Word and PDF documents, PowerPoint presentations, Excel spreadsheets, and/or images.

Figure 9.2

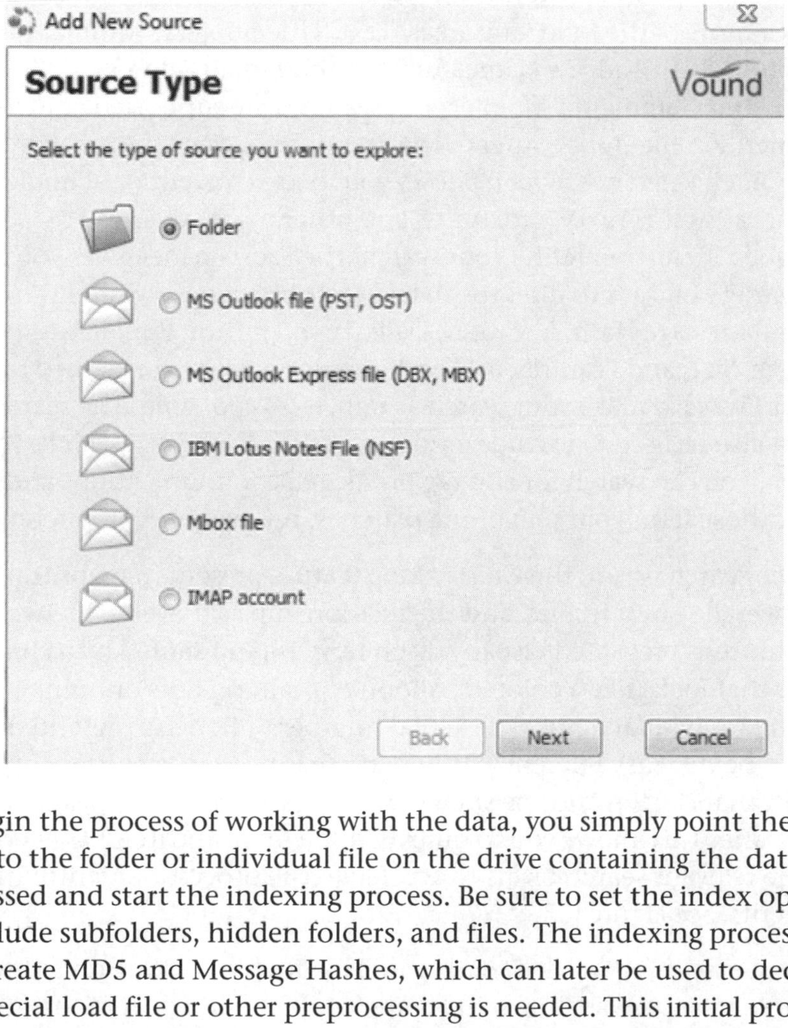

To begin the process of working with the data, you simply point the program to the folder or individual file on the drive containing the data to be processed and start the indexing process. Be sure to set the index options to include subfolders, hidden folders, and files. The indexing process will also create MD5 and Message Hashes, which can later be used to dedupe. No special load file or other preprocessing is needed. This initial process can be time consuming if you are processing large volumes of data; therefore, when dealing with many gigabytes of data, it is a good idea to start the process before you leave work with the expectation that the processing will be complete by the time you come back to work the following day. Once the indexing is complete, you can begin the process of reviewing the collection for relevant materials.

The desktop layout is straightforward. On the left side is a Search Tool panel, and below it is a Facets panel. On the right is a Cluster Map, which provides a visualization of the search results, and below it is the Details panel, which contains the data for each file in a spreadsheet format containing multiple selectable fields of data. A list, thumbnail, and timeline view area also are options in the Details panel.

To search the data, type your search query into the Search box. The box gives you the option of determining what is searched, and you can search in one or more of the following areas: Text, Title/Subject, Summary and Description, Path and File Name, Authors and E-mail Addresses, Message Headers, and Comments. Simple word searches are supported, and a dropdown menu in the right corner of the Search box opens the Keyword Search Quick Reference, which allows you to use conventional Boolean operators as well as fuzzy, proximity, and other more advanced search techniques. To further refine your search, the Facets panel gives you a broad variety of ways to filter the data. Facets include Keyword Lists, Tags, MD5 and Message Hash, Location, Date, Type, Author, E-mail Address, Language, Size, and Features, and each category can be configured in a variety of ways to make your search as targeted as possible. The search feature can also be used to exclude groups of results from your search. For example, you can search for and tag privileged communications and then exclude those from your remaining searches, reviews, and production.

Once the search is run, the Cluster Map feature presents a graphical view of the overall search results, and the relationship and overlap between the search terms is presented visually. Each term is represented by a cluster graphic that looks like a colored balloon containing dots or numbers representing individual items. The actual number of items is presented as a text number for easy reference. Where there is overlap, a cluster appears. Click on that cluster, and the smaller set of search results appears in the details pane. This allows you to quickly hone in on the items that contain multiple relevant search terms to accelerate the process of identifying key documents. See Figure 9.3.

If an item is selected in the Details panel by double clicking on a row, the Previewer will open, as shown in Figure 9.4. If you use dual monitors, you can drag the Previewer to the second monitor to increase the efficiency of your review. You can use the Previewer to view the item, view the item's header information, view its properties, check for duplicates, and tag the

Figure 9.3

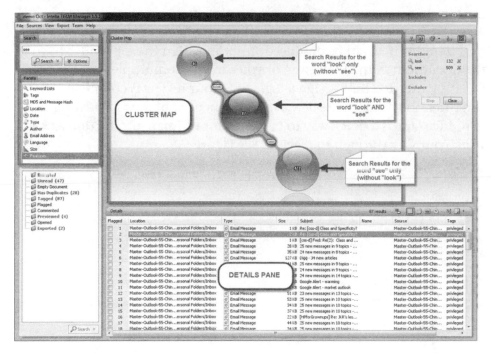

Figure 9.4

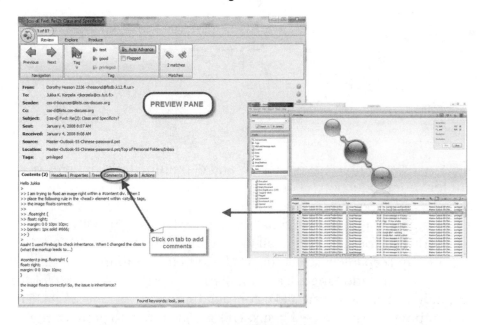

item for later production. A recent addition to the Details panel is the availability of a comments field. The user can insert comments about the item, and the comments are subsequently searchable.

As you review individual items for relevancy, you have the option of creating tags to assign to each item, and multiple tags can be assigned to a given item. You might use this technique to identify privileged or important items or items to be produced. You can assign the tag while viewing the document in the Previewer, or you can check multiple items in the Details panel and bulk assign a tag. Once your review is complete, you can filter on the tags to review a more refined set of items. Creating a "Produce" tag is a quick way to tag items for ultimate production as you work your way through the review. See Figure 9.5.

Figure 9.5

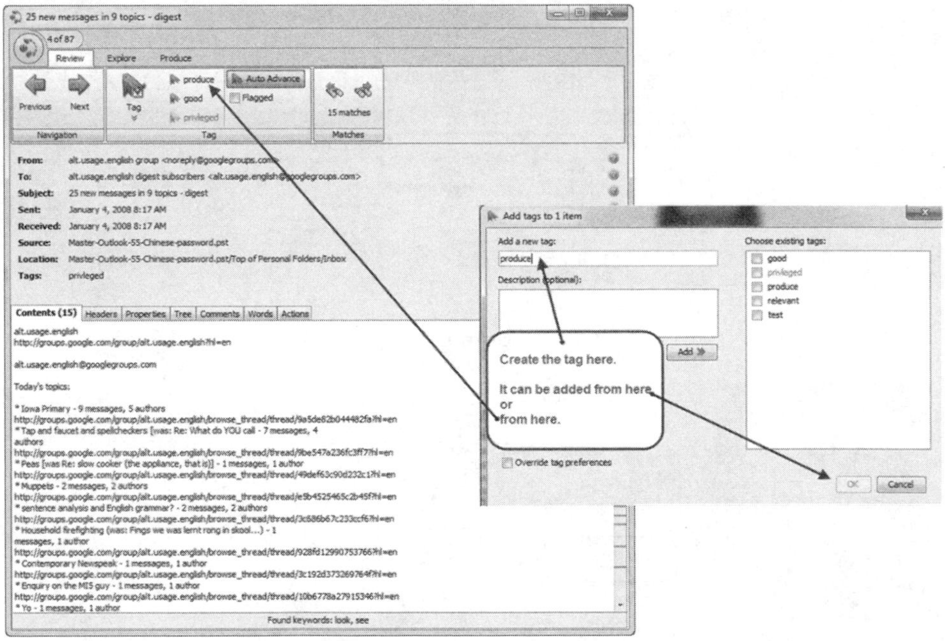

Once you have completed your review and determined which items you want for your production set or for use in a litigation support review tool, Intella has an Export wizard to help you, as set forth in Figure 9.6. There are five export options: (1) Original format (EML files); (2) PDF files (either one PDF for each item or all items combined into one PDF); (3) PST files (can keep folder structure); (4) Load files for Summation, Concordance, Relativity, and Ringtail; and (5) i2 Analyst Notebook export for further analysis. You can create a PDF for each item or create one single PDF that combines all the selected items. This is a great way to produce the electronic information in a usable electronic format if the intended recipient does not utilize any electronic litigation support. If the recipient uses electronic litigation support, and their program of choice is not available

Figure 9.6

as a specific export option, Intella will create a PST file of the results. Many of the litigation support or trial presentation programs that are in widespread use can support and convert PST files. Otherwise, service bureaus have the capability of taking a PST file and converting it into a native load file for the specific application involved.

One of the important features in Intella is the ability to search the e-mail Message ID. This is in addition to searching only the e-mail address of the sender or recipient, or by subject or date sent or received. This allows the user to track and recreate complete e-mail message threads. It can also be used to search in reverse from an e-mail backward to find the original sender of the first e-mail in an extensive thread. This can be used to prove that a given individual in fact sent an e-mail or started a particular e-mail thread. Figure 9.7 is a brief example of how Message IDs work.

There is a report wizard that can be used to create reports of the search results from the Details panel. Once you have the desired search results, you can simply right click and export the report. You can save it as a PDF or export the data as a CSV file, which can subsequently be imported into Excel or other spreadsheet programs for further manipulation. You have the option of selecting which fields to include in the export file. This technique can be used to create an MD5 hash list that can be used in filtering and deduping other data sets in other applications. See Figure 9.8.

It is also possible to export the Cluster Map as a PNG image. As Figure 9.9 illustrates, it can then be used as a demonstrative at trial if it would be useful to demonstrate how many documents in a collection contain each of the selected multiple search terms.

Figure 9.7

Original Email from Tom to Peter and Natasha NOT Chris
Message-ID: <00c301caf099$804e2d30$80ea8790$@com>
References: Nill
In-Reply-To: Nill

Reply Email from Peter to Tom and Natasha NOT Chris
Message-ID: <003601caf09f$f52a8030$df7f8090$@vound-software.com>
References: <00c301caf099$804e2d30$80ea8790$@com>
In-Reply-To: <00c301caf099$804e2d30$80ea8790$@com>

Email From Natasha to Tom, Peter and cc Chris
Message-ID:<001201caf0ba$8240d270$86c27750$@com>
References: <00c301caf099$804e2d30$80ea8790$@com>
         <003601caf09f$f52a8030$df7f8090$@vound-software.com>
In-Reply-To: <003601caf09f$f52a8030$df7f8090$@vound-software.com>

Reply Email to all from Chris
Message-ID: <4BE91FDC.3070206@aduna-software.com>
References: <00c301caf099$804e2d30$80ea8790$@com> <003601caf09f$f52a8030$df7f8090$@vound-software.com>
<001201caf0ba$8240d270$86c27750$@com>
In-Reply-To: <001201caf0ba$8240d270$86c27750$@com>

Figure 9.8

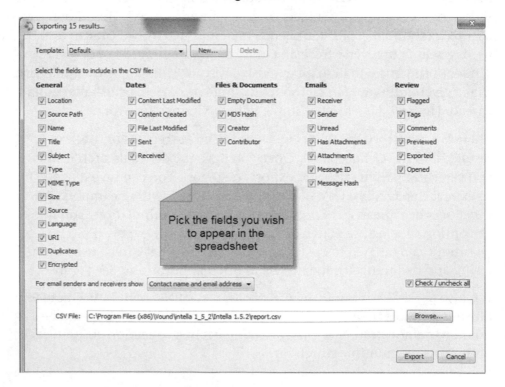

Figure 9.9

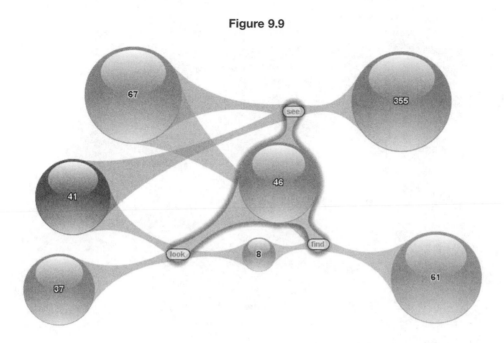

There is also a deduping feature in Intella that lets you turn the deduping feature on and off. This can be useful when reviewing a large collection to avoid the need to view each duplicate item; however, when you have created your final results set, it is a good idea to evaluate how many duplicates of the item exist as well. Intella supports full and near deduplication. Full deduplication is accomplished using MD5 hash values for files (DOC, PDF, JPG, etc.) and Message hash values for e-mail metadata and text, whereas near duplication is done using pattern analysis. Parent and child relationships can also be mapped. Intella also automatically creates an audit trail that contains a list of all user actions. Each activity is identified by user, date, and time; and a CSV file report is created that can be viewed in Excel. Finally, Intella supports multiple languages, including Asian character sets.

At the time this book was written, Intella had products starting at $1,695 per license. They have a range of products to support your needs, depending on the size of data to be analyzed and the number reviewers needed. More information is available at **www.vound-software.com**. Support is available by e-mail, and once you have registered, you also have access to Intella's support database and FAQs.

Intella offers a great solution for processing and screening large or small volumes of raw electronic data. In particular, it offers a way to assess, process, and review PST files. It provides simple to complex search capability, and the addition of visualization tools is a great assist over more traditional programs that offer only spreadsheet views.

CHAPTER TEN

Working in the Cloud

IF YOU ENGAGE IN e-discovery, even in small cases, you must have a place to store the electronic data that is collected and a place where you can work with it on a regular basis. In this day and age, it makes no sense to convert everything collected electronically to paper so you can work with it in a conventional paper-based file. Electronic files printed to paper and worked with in paper form cannot be organized into a database from which you can gain a more global view of your case. You lose the ability to key word and Boolean search to quickly access case documents. You lose access to associated metadata, such as the date a document was created or last modified. In some cases that might be extremely relevant. Therefore, you need some type of tool to manage the results of your e-discovery in either native format or as searchable electronic images of documents. Cloud-based litigation support applications are now available that are cost effective, fully functional, and easy to deploy and use. In fact, it seems likely that cloud-based applications are the future tools of preference for the storage and review of ESI in small cases.

Cloud-based litigation support and review tools have been available for a number of years. For those unfamiliar with such tools, they are basically document databases accessed over the Internet. You use your browser and a client application or program that runs as a client interface inside the browser to let you access your case data. The case data is stored securely via encryption on remote servers. The data typically is backed up several times a day to servers located at the home site and in at least one other geographical location.

This software as a service (SaaS) approach offers some significant advantages. First, it eliminates the need for an in-house IT infrastructure. This means you do not need to have file servers installed on your own network to store your case data. In fact, you do not even need to have an office network set up, which is ideal for solos and small firms. Second, it is scalable to meet your needs, so you do not need to purchase additional servers as the amount of data that needs to be stored increases. It is also easy to downgrade the amount of storage space used when a large case is over, thereby avoiding the unnecessary expense of maintaining underutilized file servers. You do not have related IT support and administrative expenses, nor do you have to manage local software installations or deal with annual software maintenance agreements. All you need is a computer and high-speed Internet access, and you are ready to go.

Until recently, the monthly storage fees for cases stored in remote SaaS databases were often too high to make these tools realistic options for small cases. Now, several products have come on the market that limit monthly storage charges to a reasonable cost of approximately $75–$250 per month for between 1 and 30 GB of data. They offer the option to buy more storage space as needed, for a reasonable additional charge per gigabyte. A rough rule of thumb is that 1 GB of data is the equivalent of seven to eight banker's boxes of imaged documents. Obviously, when data is collected and stored in native format rather than as images, significantly more data can be housed for the same cost. Because small cases in paper form typically contain between one and three banker's boxes of documents, it is reasonable to assume an average lawyer could manage all of his or her active case files for a cost of roughly $200–$400 per month.

When an annual charge of $2,400–$4,800 is compared to the annual cost of the purchase and maintenance of hardware, software, and administrative staff required to achieve and maintain the same functionality in a local area network, it is easy to see why a cloud-based solution is a very reasonable option for lawyers handling small cases. A known, regular amount charged per month is always helpful in budgeting and in managing office expenses. Furthermore, this amount can easily be divided among active cases and charged back to the clients as a monthly expense on their invoice. The ability to charge back this type of overhead is another advantage that would be difficult to replicate in an internal, networked-based setting. Clients expect the cost of servers, software, and administrative support to be part of the overhead normally covered by the hourly rate. On the other hand, a modest monthly surcharge per case for external data storage and handling is something that would be seen as the equivalent of electronic legal research, photocopying, or telephone charges that typically are billed monthly as disbursements.

The most obvious disadvantage of such a solution is that you need Internet access to access your case files. If you are going to be somewhere without hardwired or wireless Internet connectivity, you must either download local copies of the materials you intend to use while away from the office, or bring Internet connectivity with you through the use of a mobile wireless plan and wireless USB modem from your preferred cell phone provider. These days, however, connectivity issues seem easy enough to address; therefore, a cloud-based solution will be a very viable option in most cases.

Other issues to be aware of include security and ownership of client data. All cloud-based solutions have addressed security concerns through the use of encryption technology and password protection. Some products offer user level access restrictions that are even more granular than mere password protection. Given the security that comes standard with such products, the data stored on the vendor's remote servers in all probability is more secure than the data stored on your local area network protected by a consumer-grade firewall. Thus, although you must address security, it is more likely that it will not be an issue in deciding whether a cloud-based solution is right for you. The ethics of storing client data on cloud-based servers has been addressed in several jurisdictions, and the ethics opinions generally permit the use of such services so long as basic security issues have been addressed through the use of encryption and related technologies.

Other considerations include the ownership of the data, confidentiality, and what you can do if the vendor goes out of business. These types of issues usually are addressed in the service agreement. The service agreement should specify that the client owns the data, and that the vendor disclaims any ownership. The agreement should contain confidentiality provisions and should require reasonable notice of shut down to give clients the option of retrieving their data. In addition, periodic downloads by the client of their data often is recommended for backup purposes.

With the above background, let us look at several cloud-based options currently on the market that meet the needs of lawyers doing e-discovery in small cases.

Lexbe Online

The first product we will review is Lexbe Online. Lexbe Online is a Web-based litigation and document management review tool. At the time this book was written, Lexbe's Base Plan was offered at a cost of $99 per month for 1 GB of storage space, and its Firm Plan was offered at a cost of $249 per month for 10 GB of storage space. Additional storage was available at a cost of $15 per GB per month. The Base Plan includes two users; the Firm Plan includes ten users. Additional users can be added for $30 per user per month for the Base Plan and $15 per month for the Firm Plan. The plan is billed monthly with no prepayment required or penalty if you drop the service. There are no additional charges for direct online uploading or downloading. Electronic documents can be loaded as native files or as PDF files. Image PDF files are OCRed on the server. There are additional, reasonable, per-gigabyte charges for bulk handling of data when large volumes of data on disc, DVD, or external hard drive are sent to the company for processing and loading into the case database. Extra charges are also incurred for Lexbe to convert e-mail to searchable PDF files, for adding Bates stamping, for e-mail and file deduplication, and for similar services.

Lexbe's basic interface is a traditional spreadsheet. People who have worked with network-based litigation support applications like Summation, Concordance, or CaseMap will be able to quickly adapt to Lexbe. Furthermore, people who are proficient in using conventional database programs like Access or spreadsheet programs like Excel will be comfortable with Lexbe's basic layout. Lexbe supports both PCs and Macs with multiple modern browsers, without requiring additional program downloads to operate.

Lexbe stresses self-service operation; therefore, users can upload and download documents themselves, and the client account administrator can create cases and add and remove users (including regular, administrative, read-only, and limited users, such as clients or experts who can only view specified documents in a case). Support and training is available if needed.

Logging on to Lexbe is simple. Go to **www.Lexbe.com** and click on the "log in" link at the top-right side of the page. This will take you to a log-on screen where you enter your e-mail address and password. Once you have entered that information, you will be directed to the home page or dashboard. From there you can select the case you want to work in and access the various components of your case. Figure 10.1 shows the Lexbe dashboard.

The tabs across the top give access to various case components. The left side contains a number of case selection and filtering tools. The main work space contains a list of active cases.

Figure 10.1

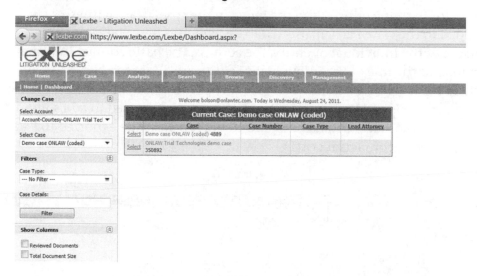

One of the strengths of Lexbe is that, in addition to providing a robust document database, it offers a number of different tools to help manage a case. The menus under the "Case" tab offer access to a Case Calendar, a Case Contacts Database, and a Case Details repository. This is also where you go to add or download documents to and from the document database.

As shown in Figure 10.2, the Case Calendar allows everyone working on the case to keep track of key dates and events, such as depositions, hearings, expert disclosures, discovery deadlines, and the like. The calendar database contains the event date and time, the event title, the event description, and the event location. Filtering options allow you to show all events, only dated events, undated events, or only future events. The calendar items can be exported to Excel to generate a master calendar written report.

Figure 10.2

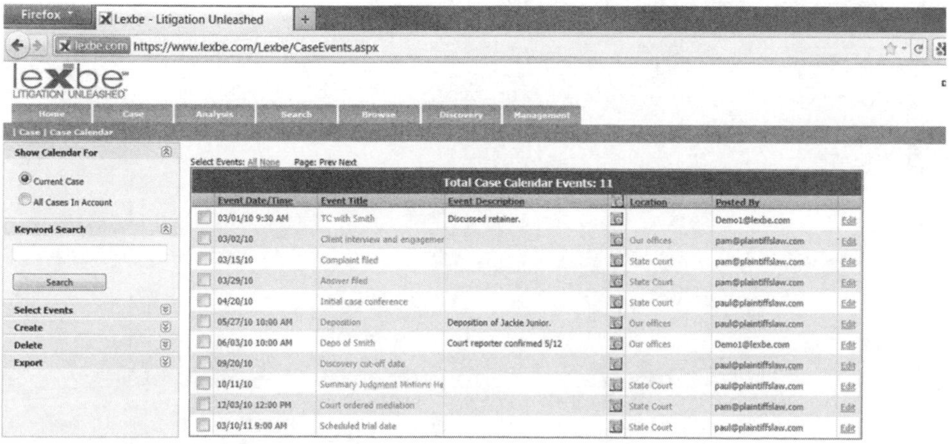

The Contacts database is a place where you can house contact information for parties, counsel, and the judge in the case. (Case witnesses are added to the Case Participants database, which is described later.) The name of the individual or entity, the address, the basic contact information, and the role of the individual or entity are all set forth in a spreadsheet view. Figure 10.3 shows an example of the spreadsheet view of all contacts, followed by Figure 10.4, a data entry screen used to add someone to the contacts database. The contents can easily be exported to Excel to generate a contacts report.

Figure 10.3

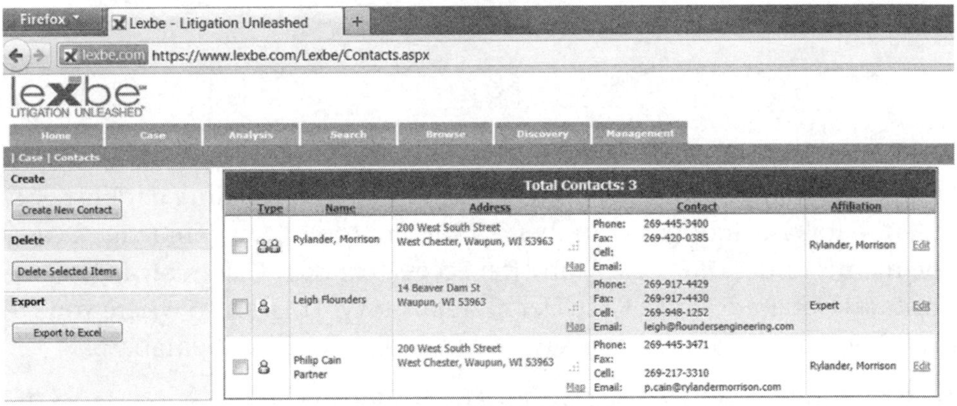

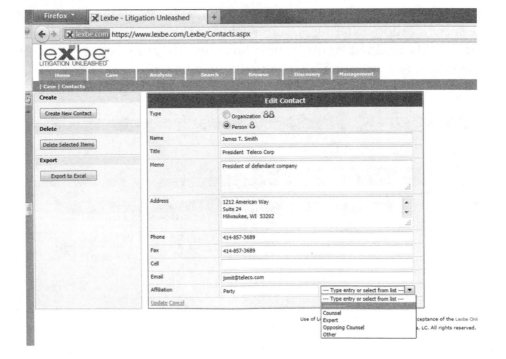

Figure 10.4

Another set of analytical tools can be found under the "Analysis" tab. Case Participants, Facts and Issues, Research, and Case Notes can all be logged in their own separate databases. The information on case participants is demonstrated in Figure 10.5. The related data entry screen is shown as Figure 10.6.

Figure 10.5

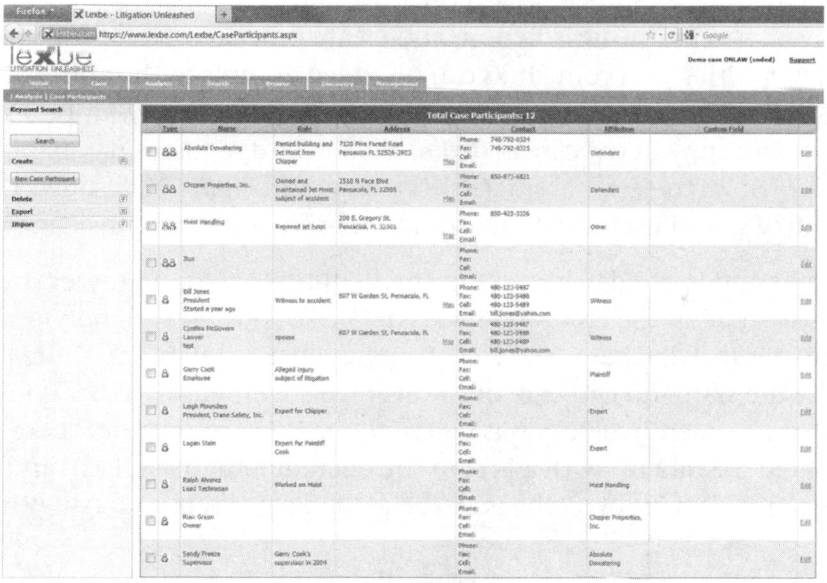

Figure 10.6

Case participants can be linked to individual case facts and issues in the Facts and Issues database.

The Research tool is another useful option that allows you to log the results of your legal research in one centralized location. From the data entry screen, you can add a topic or title for each entry, provide a summary, include a copied and pasted extraction from the legal authority, provide the name of the case and the full citation, identify the type of authority, specify the jurisdiction, and create links to full copies of the legal authorities. Full copy links can be added as links to the authority in your online case law service, to a local copy of the case on your PC or LAN, or to a copy of the case added to the Lexbe document database. Figure 10.7 shows the general spreadsheet view, and Figure 10.8 shows the data entry screen used to add information to the research spreadsheet.

The Facts and Issues database is another helpful tool found under the "Analysis" tab. In the Facts and Issues database you can add individual fact entries to a database. The fact entry includes a statement of the fact or title, the start and end date of the event, a statement whether it is contested, a statement whether it is material, a statement whether there is an associated document (with a link to the document if one exists), and a tabulated statement of all the issues related to a given fact. Sorting the

Figure 10.7

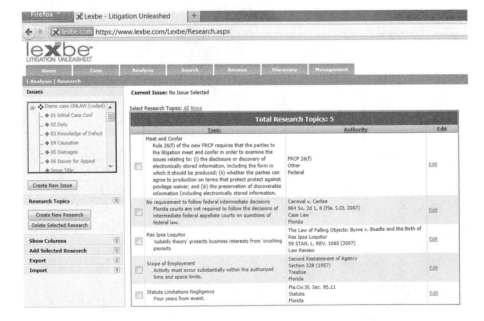

Figure 10.8

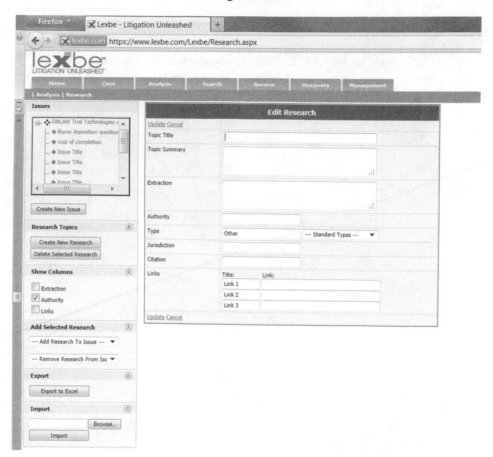

information by date will give you a complete case chronology of facts. You can also build an issues outline of pertinent issues in the case. You can associate individual facts with one or more issues and then filter on a particular issue to view just the facts that are related to the specified issue. It is also possible to search by key word within the database and use multiple filter options to drill down your output to only the facts and issues of interest.

Figure 10.9 shows a Facts and Issues database containing sixty-nine facts. Note the issue outline in the upper left corner. Below it is a Keyword Search box and a number of different filters you can use to limit the data that is displayed. On the right is the fact spreadsheet sorted in reverse chronological order. Figure 10.10 shows the data entry screen for adding information to the Facts and Issues database.

Figure 10.9

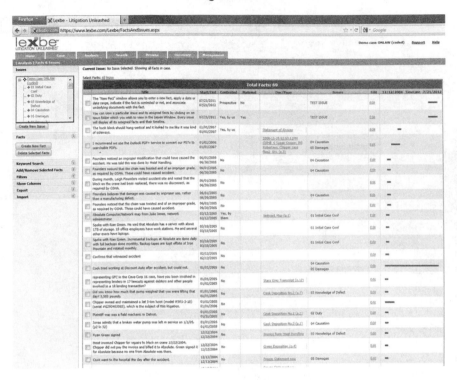

Figure 10.10

Another feature of the "Analysis" tab is the Case Notes database. Users with access to the case can enter notes, thoughts and comments, assignments, follow-up items, etc. These notes can stand alone or be associated with documents in the document database. In the spreadsheet view, you can view notes containing a case note title, a note description, a reference to the page of the document that is the subject of the note, the date and time the note was created, the identity of the person who created the note, and the link to the document in the document database. The notes themselves are searchable by key word. The notes can be shared among the team working on the case, or they can be limited to only a given user. Figure 10.11 shows the Case Notes database.

Figure 10.11

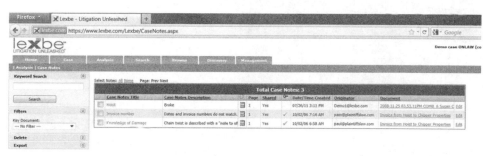

The primary feature of Lexbe is, of course, the document database. The case documents can be accessed globally from the "Browse" tab. A spreadsheet view is presented. A variety of pre-existing coded fields exists for each document, and you can add an unlimited number of custom fields. All fields are visible as you move across a row of the spreadsheet. The visible columns can be defined by the user by clicking on the "Show Columns" button on the left. The data can be sorted and filtered by any of the different fields. In addition to being an item identified by the data in the row within the spreadsheet, Lexbe has the ability to assign documents to folders. The Folder Quick Links are located on the left side of the screen, and by clicking on a listed folder, you can quickly focus on only the documents assigned to that specific folder. This feature is particularly useful for people who are used to using nested folders in Windows Explorer for organizing information. Figure 10.12 is an example of a page in the document database accessed from the "Browse" tab.

To view a given document, simply double click on the link in the Title field, and the document viewer is launched. A separate browser tab is opened for the viewer. This is convenient for those who use dual monitors. You can place the viewer on one monitor screen and the spreadsheet on the other. An example of an e-mail visible in the viewer is set forth in Figure 10.13.

Figure 10.12

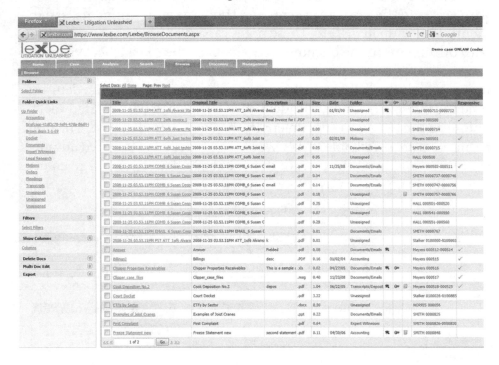

Figure 10.13

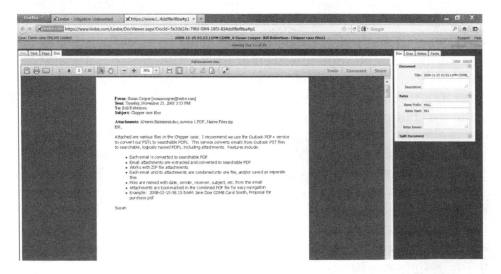

Note that, in addition to viewing the document, you have a series of windows on the right side that allow you to code and tag the document. Figure 10.13 shows the Doc view; Figure 10.14 shows the Discovery view.

Figure 10.14

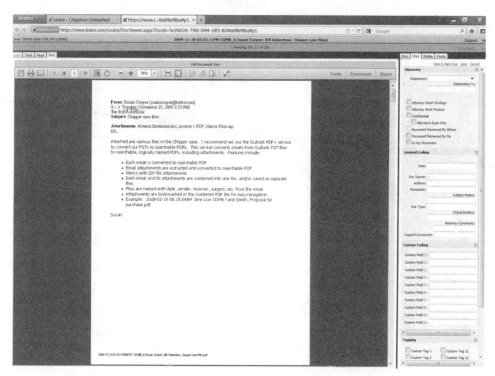

Note the many different standard and customizable fields that can be utilized to assign data fields as descriptors of the document.

Figure 10.15 shows the Notes view, and this is where the viewers can make their notes related to a given document. Notes can be viewed when looking at a given document, or the entire set of notes can be viewed in the Notes database discussed above.

Lexbe uses the tools under the "Discovery" tab to create production sets. Search the database for the documents that you want to produce and assign them to a given production set. Figure 10.16 shows the search results for documents that are not privileged and not work product. Assuming you want to produce these documents, you can use the options on the left to add Bates numbers and determine which columns to view in the spreadsheet. You can then create the production set and use the spreadsheet view as a production log. A similar search for privileged documents can be run to generate a privilege log.

Figure 10.15

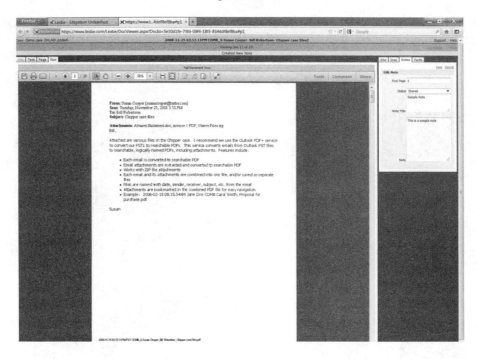

Figure 10.16

There are many additional features that will benefit an advanced user of Lexbe that are not covered in this chapter; however, the above should give you a good overview of Lexbe with an understanding of its current cost. It is clear that a full-featured, cloud-based litigation support tool is available to you for a modest cost. Lexbe is one of several options that are ideal for working with the results of e-discovery generated in small cases.

Nextpoint Discovery Cloud and Trial Cloud

Another reasonably priced option is Nextpoint's Discovery Cloud and Trial Cloud. Nextpoint offers a somewhat different approach to managing ESI in the cloud. It offers two, low-cost integrated solutions: Discovery Cloud and Trial Cloud, and each focuses on a separate phase of litigation. Discovery Cloud is a litigation support database that is used to house, code, review, and produce case-related documents. Trial Cloud holds the items that are deemed relevant to the trial and trial preparation of the case. Relevant items in the Discovery Cloud database are transferred to a separate Trial Cloud database, which contains the document database along with deposition and trial transcript management tools.

Despite the fact that there are two modules available, a Nextpoint annual subscription includes both products for a single fee based on a monthly charge. The base plan is the Team Plan. At the time this book was written, Nextpoint's Team Plan was offered at a cost of $75 per month for 15 GB of storage space, and its Group Plan was offered at a cost of $150 per month for 30 GB of storage space. The Pro Plan was offered at a cost of $250 per month for 50 GB of storage space. Additional storage is available through the Unlimited Plan at a cost of $25 per GB per month. The Team Plan includes five users; the Group Plan ten users; the Pro Plan fifteen users; the Unlimited plan an unlimited number of users. All plans are annual contract plans, and the full amount for the year is due upon signing of the contract. The Unlimited Plan is month to month. There are no additional charges for direct online uploading or downloading of documents. Electronic documents can be loaded as native files or as PDF files. OCRing of the loaded PDF files is included in the base charge. There are additional services that are available for an additional charge, including deduplication, key word extraction, date restriction, analyzing and populating relevant metadata fields, bulk importing or exporting of data, and assistance with production management.

Discovery Cloud
Discovery Cloud's basic interface is modeled on a Google-type interface rather than on a conventional spreadsheet view of a case database. Thus,

for users who are not proficient with spreadsheet-based programs, but are familiar with searching the Internet through Google, this might be a natural fit. Those used to working with databases in spreadsheet mode might take a short time to acclimate to this different approach.

Logging on to Discovery Cloud is simple. Go to **www.nextpoint.com** and click on the customer login at the bottom left of the page. This will link to a log-on screen in which you enter your e-mail address and password. For further security, each computer that is used for access must be registered using a registration number that is provided by e-mail to your personal e-mail account. Once you have entered that information, select whether you want to work in the Discovery Cloud or Trial Cloud database by making a selection from the drop-down list at the top. After you select "Discovery Cloud," you will be directed to the search page as set forth in Figure 10.17.

Figure 10.17

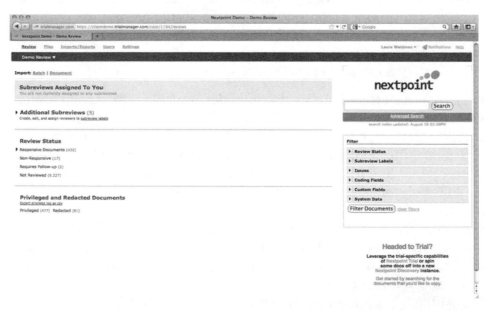

The Discovery Cloud search page includes a variety of information about the documents that have been loaded into your database, including what items were assigned to which reviewer, whether items remain to be reviewed and coded, how many documents have been tagged as responsive or nonresponsive, and whether any documents need additional review by a higher-level reviewer. Filtering tools on the right side of the screen allow you to filter by review status, by sub-review labels (which include groups of documents assigned to different reviewers in a multi-reviewer situation), by issue, or by several other filtering options.

In addition to filtering, you can jump right into the database by searching single terms in the search term window on the right-hand side of the screen or by selecting "Advanced Search" and using the available wizard to create a more complex Boolean search. A search of the term "contract" generated the results screen set forth as Figure 10.18.

Figure 10.18

In this instance there were 347 matches found. They are presented like Google search results, ranked by text relevance. You have the option to change the sort criteria to sort by Bates Number, Shortcut, Subject/Title, Document Date, Author, and a variety of e-mail related fields.

Once you have found a document you want to review, click on the hyperlink in the title, and the document viewer is launched. The viewer opens in a new browser page so it can be moved to a second monitor if you are using dual monitors. You can view the document in the viewer, as set forth below, have a PDF copy e-mailed to you, or launch Adobe Acrobat and view the document in its native application. Figure 10.19 shows an e-mail displayed in the viewer. Note that, in addition to the e-mail itself in the view pane on the left, a variety of coded information and document-related metadata is available on the right side of the screen.

Figure 10.19

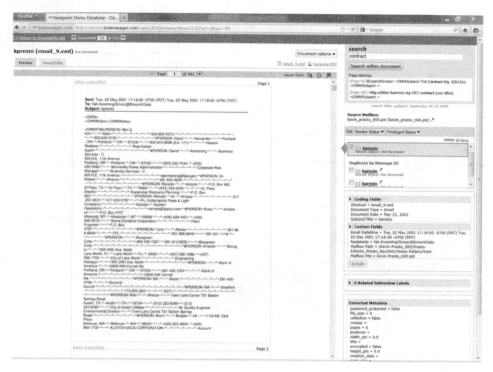

The foregoing results were based on a single word search using the term "contract." More advanced Boolean searching is available using the "Advanced Search" tab. Figure 10.20 shows the "Advanced Search" tab

Figure 10.20

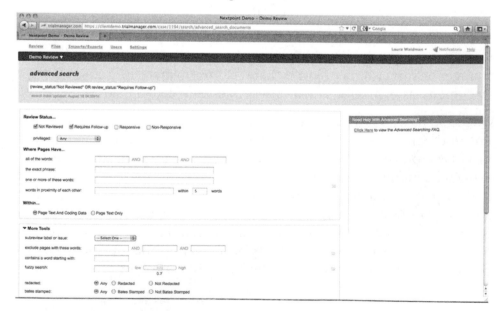

where the user is searching for all unreviewed documents or documents that need further review. A variety of options are available in this wizard to help you build multiple, complex Boolean searches.

Adding new documents to the database is a straightforward process. To add a single document, go to the "Import/Export" tab and select "Upload a new single document," as shown in Figure 10.21. An upload window opens, and you can browse to the local location of the document to be loaded. You can add a shortcut name and the subject/title of the document at the time of upload. Duplicate documents will automatically be detected to avoid loading the same document on multiple occasions. This option can be disabled on a document-by-document basis by selecting the disable feature.

Figure 10.21

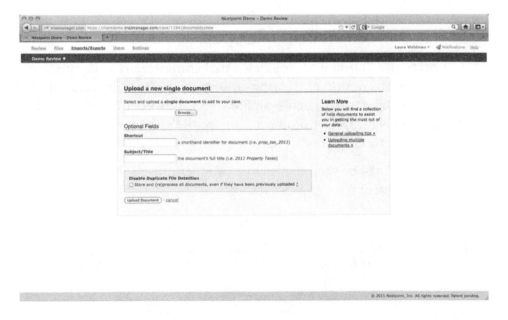

A similar process is used to load batches of documents. The batch must first be zipped before you browse to the ZIP file you want to batch and click on "Create Batch." See Figure 10.22.

Once documents have been added to the database, they must be coded. Coding of a document occurs as follows:

1. Select the document you wish to code and open it in the viewer.

2. On the right side of the screen the Coding Fields are visible.

3. Click on the Coding Fields drop-down arrow to select the fields you wish to edit.

Figure 10.22

In addition to the standard coding fields that come as part of the program, you have the option of creating custom fields. Custom fields can be edited just like the standard fields. Figure 10.23 shows coding for the standard fields, and Figure 10.24 shows coding for the custom fields. Once coding is complete, click the "Update" button to save your changes.

Discovery Cloud can be used to generate production sets for electronic distribution of documents that are responsive to a particular discovery

Figure 10.23

Figure 10.24

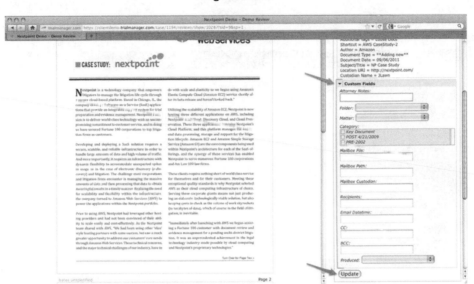

request. As you search the database for potentially relevant items, you code those that are responsive and then filter to generate a search results set of only the documents to be produced.

The first step is to create a responsive issue for the production set. Select the "Responsive Issues" tab from the Settings drop-down menu. Click on "Add New" to open the New Issue data entry screen. Figures 10.25 and 10.26 show this process.

Figure 10.25

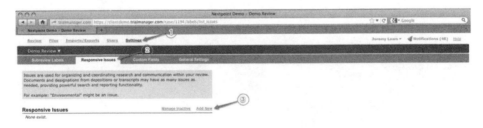

Figure 10.26

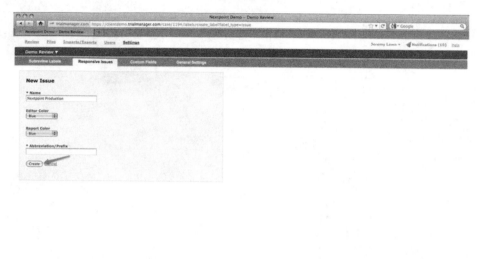

The next step is to search for documents to add to the responsive issue. In this case "contract" was searched, and it yielded 347 results. See Figure 10.27.

Figure 10.27

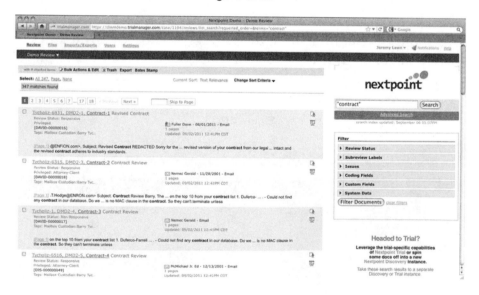

Now the selected items can be bulk coded as responsive by linking them to the issue. At the top of the search results screen is a "Bulk Actions & Edit" tab (see Figure 10.28). This is selected, and the Bulk Edit window appears (see Figure 10.29). Select "Set Review Status" as "Responsive," then select the sub-issue to which it is responsive and click on "Update Documents."

Figure 10.28

Figure 10.29

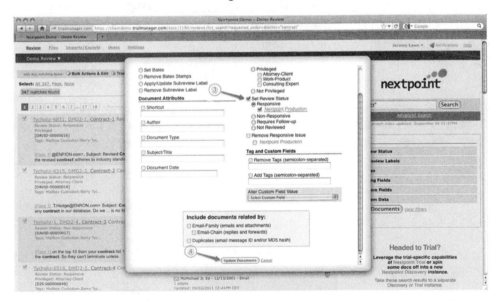

The document set is available on the home page under Review Status/ Responsive Documents/Production Ready. See Figure 10.30. It can be Bates stamped, exported, or reproduced as a document set. The exported document set can be downloaded locally and then copied to a CD/DVD or to an external memory device for delivery to the intended recipient.

Figure 10.30

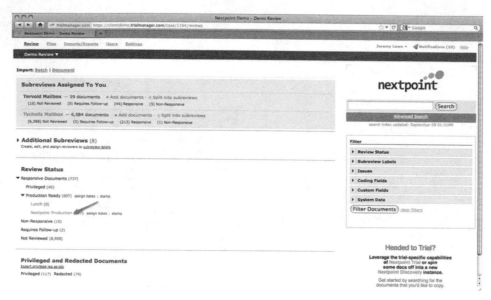

A similar process is followed to copy the items you deem relevant for trial into the Trial Cloud companion database. Figure 10.31 shows a search results screen with the Export drop-down expanded. To copy to Trial Cloud, select "Copy to Another Instance."

Figure 10.31

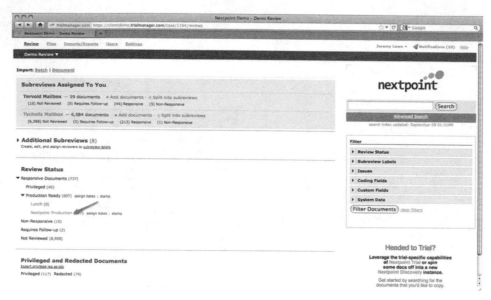

That selection will generate another screen that gives you the option to create a new case in Trial Cloud or to copy the items to an existing case. See Figure 10.32.

Figure 10.32

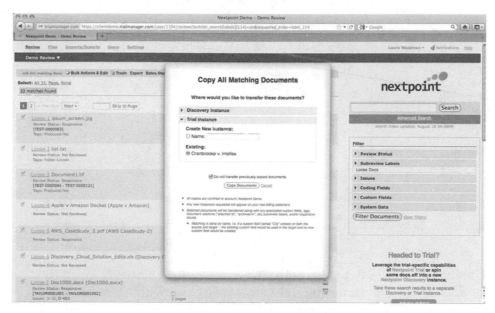

A record will be created within Discovery Cloud of the export job you have created identifying the batch that was exported, the date and time it was exported, and the user who initiated the export. This status information can be found on the home page. Once this process is finished, you are ready to work with the relevant items in Trial Cloud.

Trial Cloud

Trial Cloud's basic interface is also modeled on a Google-type interface rather than on a conventional spreadsheet view of the case database. Logging on is simple. Go to **www.nextpoint.com** and click on the customer login at the bottom left of the page. This will link to a log-on screen on which you enter your e-mail address and password. For further security, each computer that is used for access must be registered using a registration number that is provided by e-mail. Once you have entered that information, you will be directed to the Search page. From there you can immediately begin searching the case or select from one of the bread crumbs at the top of the page to go directly to the case database, to depositions, to transcripts, and more.

Figure 10.33

The initial screen after sign in, the Search screen, is set forth as Figure 10.33. You can start working right away using the Search function. Basic searching is simple and is similar to Google searching. In Figure 10.33 under the "Search" tab, the word "contract" is inserted as the search term, and the search will be conducted across all the case evidence. You do have the option to limit the search to only documents, depositions, or transcripts. Running the search generates a search results screen that sets forth each responsive item ranked by relevance, just like a Google search result. See Figure 10.34.

Note that each hit contains a variety of descriptive information in addition to the item's title. It also gives you the option to click and view the item in the document viewer, launch it in theater mode, view it as a native PDF to be viewed in Acrobat, or have it e-mailed to you as a PDF attachment. The document in the program viewer appears as Figure 10.35.

Note that, in addition to a rendered view of the document on the left side of the screen, information about the document is available on the right side of the screen. This includes a recap of the search term, designation labels, issues, document metadata, and custom coded field data.

Figure 10.34

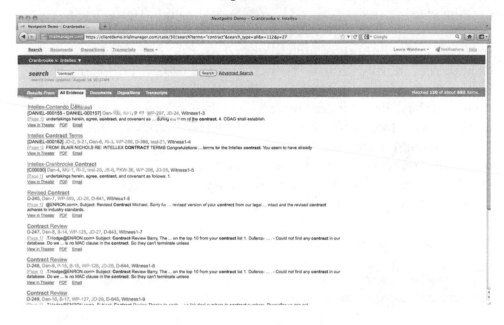

Figure 10.35

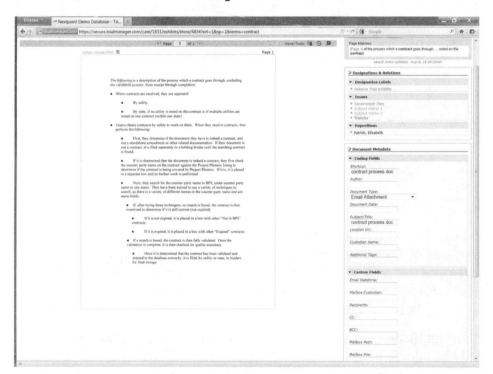

In addition to simple key word searching, more complex searches can be developed using the "Advanced Search" tab shown in Figure 10.36. You can limit the databases in which you search to only documents or transcripts. You can limit the search to several words, a certain phrase, or exclude certain words. You can search only the text of the document or include both the text and the coded data. You can limit the search to items that have been tagged with certain labels or issues. You can even do a fuzzy search. In essence, the "Advanced Search" tab is a wizard that helps you build more complex Boolean searches. As you use the wizard over time, you will educate yourself on Boolean search syntax so that eventually you will be able create advanced search strings directly without the need to use the wizard.

Figure 10.36

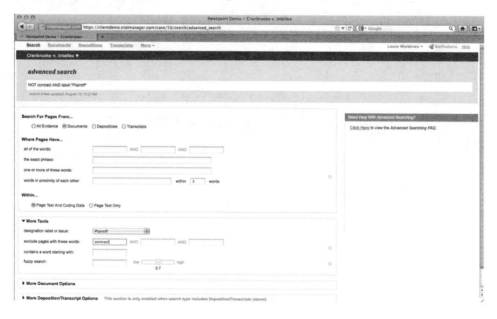

You can also search from the "Documents" tab using the Filter bar on the right side of the screen. This allows you to quickly pull up all items that have been designated with a particular label or issue. Figure 10.37 is the search from the Documents tab, filtering on the designation label "TEST." Figure 10.38 is the search results screen.

It is a simple process to add documents to the database. They can obviously be added from the Discovery Cloud database using the export tools in Discovery Cloud. You can also upload a single document or use a ZIP file to batch load multiple documents directly into your Trial Cloud case.

Figure 10.37

Figure 10.38

Figure 10.39 shows the view for uploading a single document. Use the Browse function to locate the document on your computer. You can optionally add a shortcut identifier and a subject or title. Click "Upload Document," and the document is added to the case database.

Figure 10.39

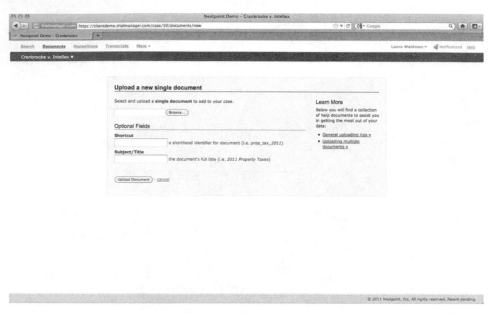

In addition to the document database, Trial Cloud can be used to manage deposition transcripts. Figure 10.40 shows all of the depositions that have been entered into the case database. The list of deponents in alphabetical order is located on the left side of the screen. The Filter bar on the right

Figure 10.40

identifies the designation labels and issues that have been assigned. You can filter by labels or issues within a given deposition or across multiple depositions. You can search for specified words in a deposition and jump to the places in the transcript where the word is found. In addition to providing the text of the deposition, Trial Cloud also supports synchronized video that can be played back within the program.

In Figure 10.41, the transcripts were first filtered by label, and defense depositions were selected. Elizabeth Patrick's deposition was then selected. Next, the word "intersection" was searched with the resulting output. Note that the search within the deposition resulted in two pages of hits. The search results are set forth immediately below the search term window and above the video player. You have the further option of launching the video playback in full-screen mode by selecting "View In Theater" from the "More options" drop-down menu.

Figure 10.41

Adding a deposition or transcript to the database is similar to adding a document. Figure 10.42 shows the process for adding a single deposition; Figure 10.43 shows the process for adding multiple depositions at one time.

Similar functionality exists for viewing trial or hearing transcripts. The text files from the court reporter for daily trial transcripts or motion hearings can be loaded into the program and then be viewed, searched, and filtered just like deposition transcripts. See Figure 10.44.

Figure 10.42

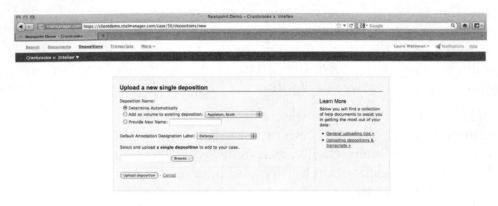

Figure 10.43

Another unique feature of Trial Cloud is the Theater Mode. This can be used as a trial presentation tool in court or in mediation. A selection from the search results generated the view shown in Figure 10.45 in the document viewer.

Figure 10.44

Figure 10.45

Launching this same document in Theater Mode gives the view set forth in Figure 10.46. The document is launched by clicking on the "View in Theater" option under the "Document options" drop-down menu.

Figure 10.46

Documents can be annotated in a number of different ways. First, you can select an area to create a zoomed callout. See Figure 10.47. Simply click and drag the region you want to appear in the callout.

Figure 10.47

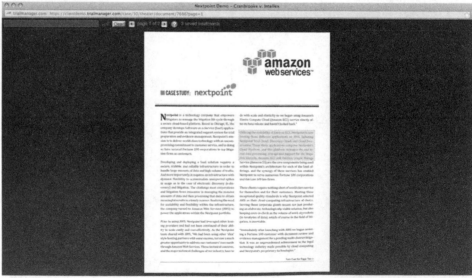

The selected region will expand, as shown in Figure 10.48. Once that has occurred, you can annotate further by highlighting, underlining, or whiting out selected text. Figure 10.49 contains both highlighting and underlining.

Figure 10.48

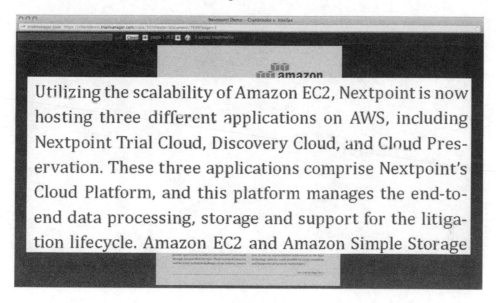

Figure 10.49

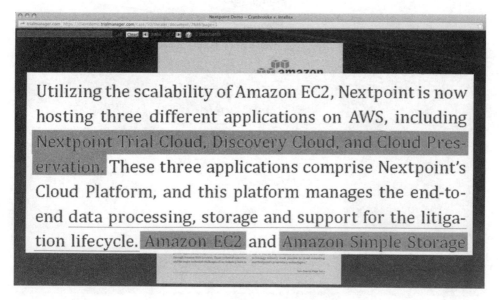

The annotations can be saved. See Figure 10.50.

A single document may have multiple treatments, which are accessed by selecting the desired thumbnail. See Figure 10.51.

Multipage document treatments containing each step of the process can be created and saved for later playback in court or in mediation. See Figure 10.52.

Figure 10.50

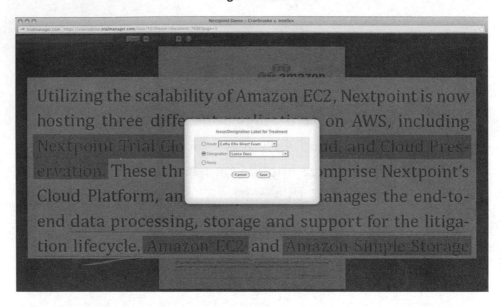

Figure 10.51

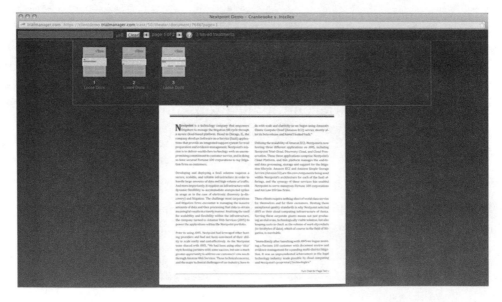

Figure 10.52

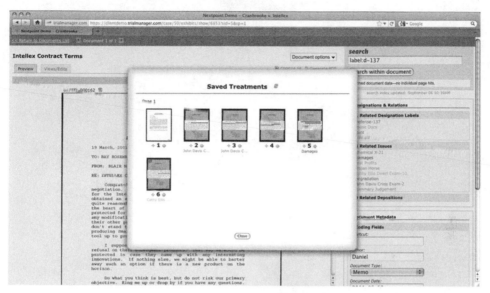

Given the modest cost for storage of data, Nextpoint's Discovery Cloud and Trial Cloud is another viable cloud-based solution for storing and working with the ESI you generate as part of e-discovery in small cases. The Google-type searching functionality and basic interface makes these products particularly well suited to new users of litigation support software who have not become accustomed to the traditional spreadsheet mode of viewing database information.

CHAPTER ELEVEN

A Simple Solution for Producing ESI

A GREAT DEAL OF attention is paid to the collecting, processing, and reviewing of ESI. Much less attention is given to the production of the results of such efforts, particularly when you are looking for an easy-to-use tool that can create a set of documents that can be viewed and searched by anyone. If the intended recipient of these electronic files has no litigation support program available, what can you do to provide deliverables that are immediately usable? dtSearch Publish is a tool that lets you quickly publish a document collection to a CD, DVD, or portable hard drive that is instantly searchable by the recipient using dtSearch Publish's powerful search engine technology. What is more is that the recipient does not even need to have dtSearch Publish installed on his or her computer to be able to use it to search the documents on the CD, DVD, or external memory device you provide. The search capabilities are automatically built into the CD, DVD, or hard drive, requiring no software installation on the recipient's hard drive.

dtSearch Publish

To create your dtSearch Publish collection on a CD, DVD, or external hard drive, a simple wizard is used. See Figure 11.1. All you need to do is follow the steps and you will easily create a usable end product. Click on the "New CD" button on the wizard to designate a master folder on your hard drive to hold the files until they are burned to CD, DVD, or external drive. Once you have created the target, add the documents you want to produce. You have the option of adding individual files using Explorer to copy the files into the documents folder or to copy items in bulk using the "Add Folder" command. See Figure 11.2.

Figure 11.1

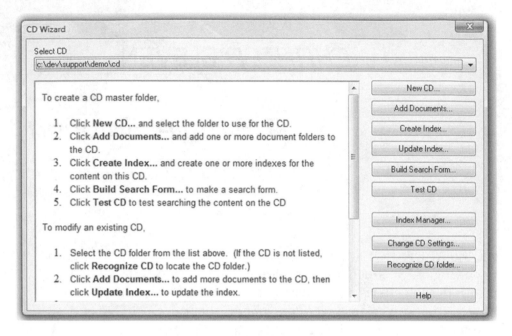

Figure 11.2

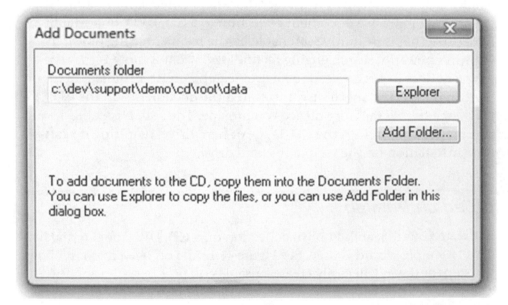

Once you have added the documents you want to produce, it is necessary to create an index. When you click on the "Create Index" button, you must name the index file, specify a location for it to be created, and then decide whether a summary or a detailed report is in order. A detailed report will list all files indexed. Advanced features give you the option to cache document text or documents in the index and specify the fields to display in the search results. Sticking with the default settings, however, makes this a simple two-click process.

After creating the index, add the documents to the index. More advanced features are once again available, and you can choose to index only a particular file or folder, add items from an Outlook folder or the Web, or apply file filters to exclude certain types of files by extension. Once you have set the indexing parameters, the indexing process is started. When complete, the results screen allows you to view the log if desired.

The next step in the wizard is to create a search form. Again, the default can be used or you can customize the form in a variety of more advanced ways. See Figures 11.3 through 11.6.

Figure 11.3

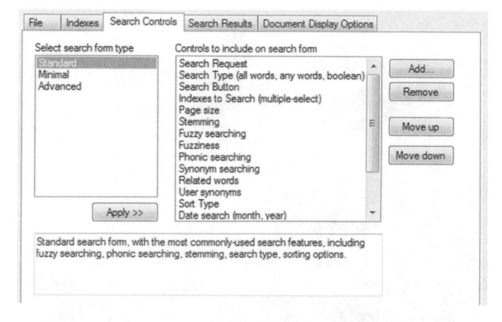

Figure 11.4

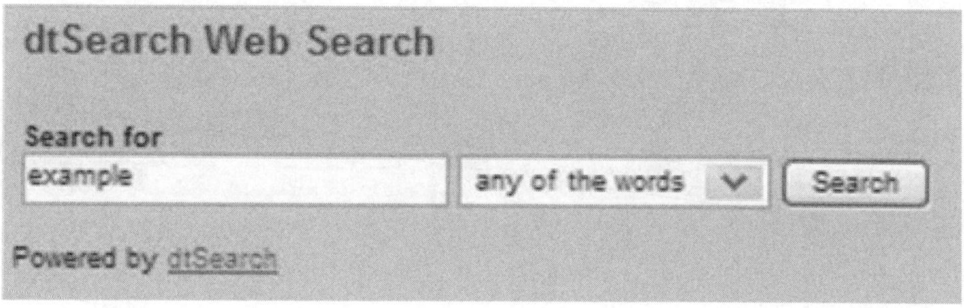

Figure 11.5

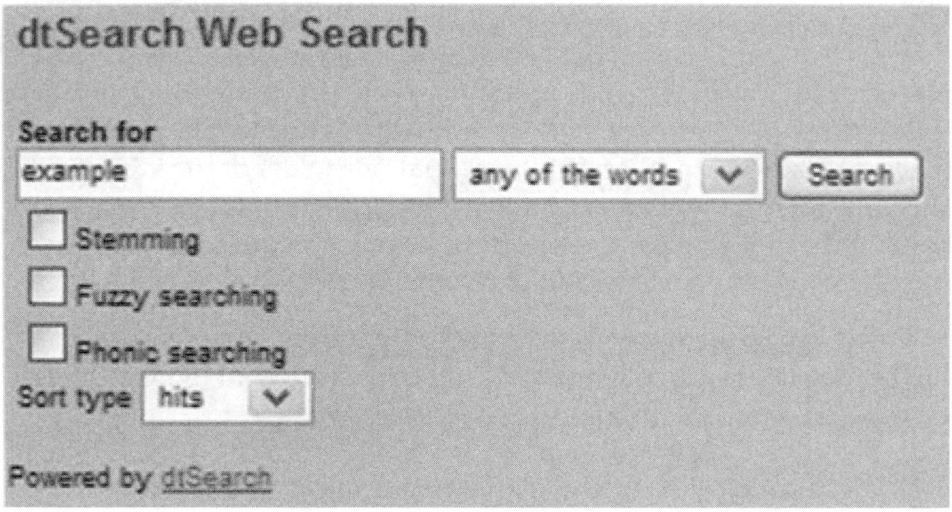

> ## dtSearch Web Search
>
> **Search for**
>
> example   any of the words ▾   Search
>
> ☐ Stemming
> ☐ Fuzzy searching
> ☐ Phonic searching
> Sort type hits ▾
>
> Powered by dtSearch

Figure 11.6

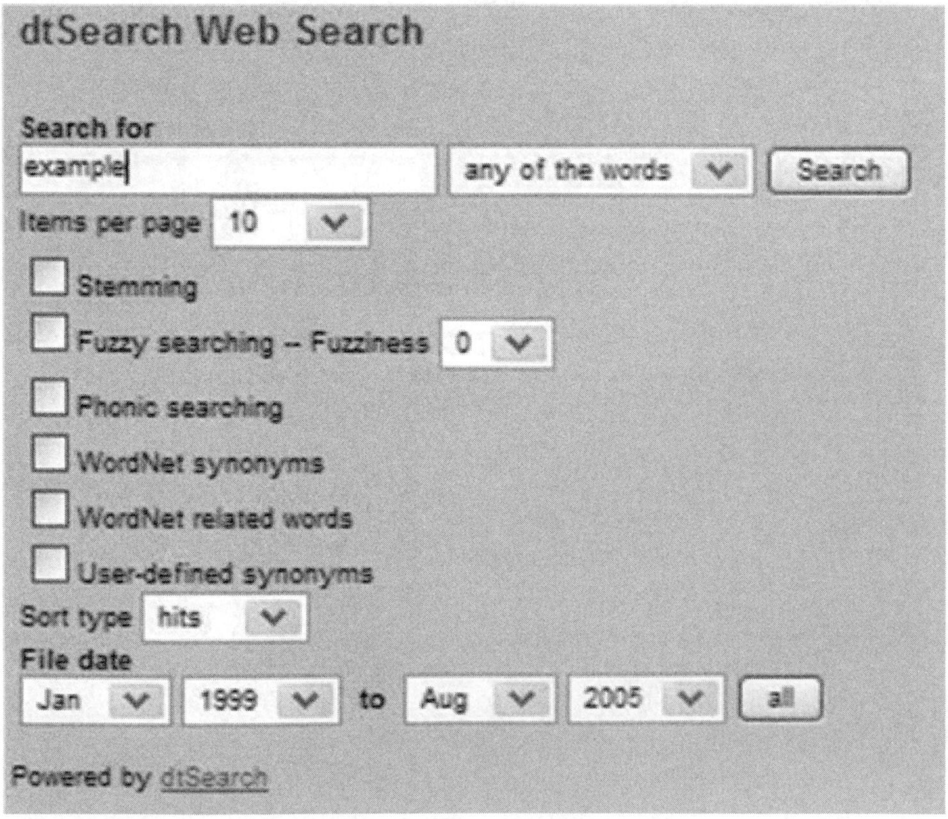

> ## dtSearch Web Search
>
> **Search for**
>
> example   any of the words ▾   Search
> Items per page 10 ▾
>
> ☐ Stemming
> ☐ Fuzzy searching -- Fuzziness 0 ▾
> ☐ Phonic searching
> ☐ WordNet synonyms
> ☐ WordNet related words
> ☐ User-defined synonyms
> Sort type hits ▾
> **File date**
> Jan ▾ 1999 ▾ to Aug ▾ 2005 ▾ all
>
> Powered by dtSearch

Finally, you are ready to test the collection on the CD, DVD, or external drive. Assuming it tests correctly, that is all there is to it. Although you have the option of further customization, using the default settings for this simple five-step process will create everything you need to burn a CD, DVD, or create a copy on an external hard drive. The burning process is done using your default burning software.

Delivering ESI That Is Universally Viewable and Searchable

Turning now to the end result, what kind of deliverable would you receive if you were the on the other side? The process is simple. You would place the CD or DVD you received in the appropriate drive, or you would attach the external memory device to your computer and launch the program. You are directed to the Search page in what looks like a Web browser with two panes: a search pane and a results pane, with a tool bar across the top. See Figure 11.7. This interface is very easy to use. The tool bar at the top of the page allows you to quickly access the Search page to begin a new search, to print, or to move backward and

Figure 11.7

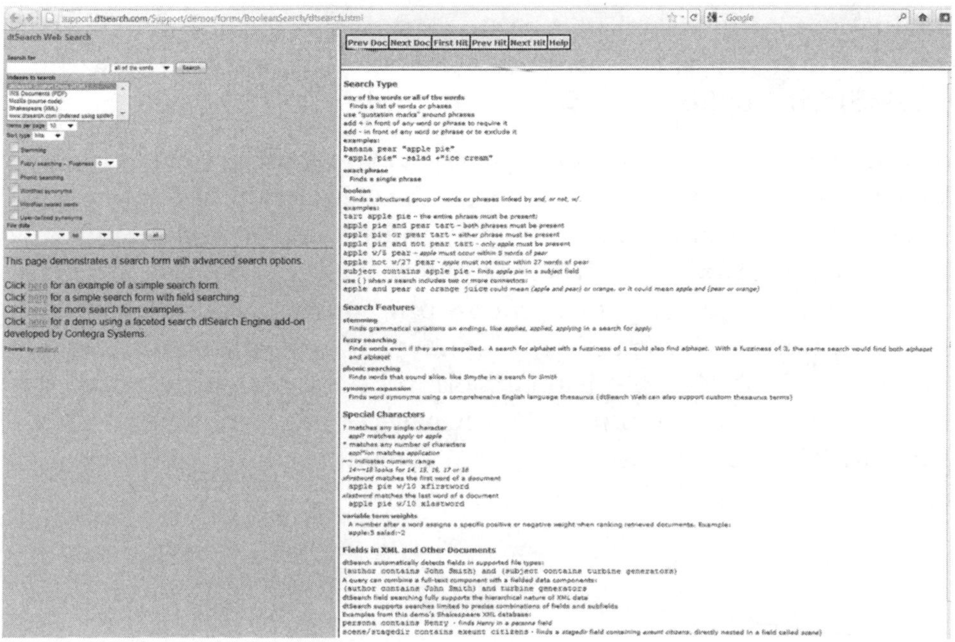

forward between the pages on which you have been working. When you first open the program, before you have begun a search, the opening page includes search instructions and hints for successful use of the program. There is also an extensive help menu that provides additional instruction where needed.

The opening view presents a "Search for" field on the left side of the page where you enter the words or phrases you want searched. A drop down menu gives you the option of searching for all the words, any of the words, the exact phrase, or you can use Boolean search terms and techniques. You can also select whether stemming, fuzzy, or phonic searching should be included. Finally, you have the option to organize the hit list by number of hits, date, name, or size of the file.

Once you have entered your search terms and run the search, you will have data appearing in the search results list below the search box. Each box displays a hot link to a document using the document's file name, along with additional information about the document based on the display fields that were specified by the person who created the CD, DVD, or external drive. The default result includes the number of hits, the date, the size of the file, and the title of the document. If you left click on the highlighted link to the document, the document will be viewable in the viewer in the right-hand pane. The viewer technology that is used gives you a rendered view that looks like the original, but you do not need the original application installed to be able to view the document. Using buttons on the viewer pane, you can navigate quickly from hit to hit within the document, or from document to document.

Assuming you have found a document that you want to copy for further analysis and use, you can right click on the viewer pane and select from several options. First, you can highlight individual text and simply copy and paste it into another document, or do a copy all and paste. You can also print the document. If you choose print preview, you will access several options for formatting the result you want to print. You can turn headers and footers on and off, print the full page with the search results and viewer both printed on the page, or print only the selected pane, which would give you just the document result or the search results.

At the time this book was written, a single location e-discovery license of dtSearch Publish cost approximately $3,500 per year. dtSearch Publish is easy to use, both for the creator of the CD, DVD, or external hard drive and the recipient. It is a great solution to creating a production set of ESI that is immediately usable by the recipient. No specialized litigation software is needed, and no advanced IT support is required to access the contents of the CD, DVD, or external drive. dtSearch Publish is an ideal tool for lawyers who must produce ESI in discovery for other lawyers who lack other litigation support capabilities.

CHAPTER TWELVE

Managing E-Mail with Adobe Acrobat Portfolios

IT IS NOT UNUSUAL in small cases to find yourself dealing with e-mail files as a single category of ESI. It is often possible to determine at the outset of a case that only e-mail is relevant; therefore, you only need a tool that will allow you to process and review e-mail files and attachments. This typically will involve the production of PST files for several custodians who use Outlook as their e-mail client. Lotus Notes is another common e-mail client that you might also encounter. For purposes of our discussion, however, we will focus on Outlook (although the Adobe Acrobat Portfolio solution for dealing with e-mail that we discuss later applies to both programs).

Adobe Acrobat

Many of you already have the software available in your office, although typically you have not thought of it as an e-discovery tool. Adobe Acrobat X (or its earlier version, Adobe Acrobat 9) offers a reasonable solution for capturing, reviewing, and producing e-mail as part of e-discovery, particularly when you are dealing with small collections. Acrobat can be used to create an e-mail portfolio out of an e-mail folder in Outlook or Lotus Notes. The portfolio is searchable and can be filtered by date, sender, recipient, and other fields. Individual e-mails are converted to PDF. Attachments in their native format are added to the PDF. All of the converted messages are combined into a single PDF portfolio. In the conversion process, a full-text index is added to the portfolio. The portfolio can then be copied and produced to other parties in the lawsuit.

In addition to Adobe Acrobat, you must have Outlook installed on the PC you use for processing. The conversion process also requires some customized set up of Outlook so that you can import the PST and MSG files that are to be produced into the Outlook program installed on the processing machine. It is useful to create a new user account specifically to use for processing e-discovery e-mail files. You do not want to mix up the e-mail files to be processed with the e-mail that may exist in the normal user account for the person who regularly uses the PC you are using for processing. For detailed instructions on setting up the user account and for loading the e-mail file into the new user account, see **http://blogs.adobe.com/ acrolaw/2009/11/creating-email-for-small-edd-productions**.

Once the files are properly loaded into a folder in Outlook, the conversion process to create PDF files is simple. From Outlook, choose the Adobe PDF drop-down menu and select "Convert Selected Folders." Then select "Create New PDF." The Conversion Window opens, and you select the folder or folders to process. In this case, you would select the special administrator's account you set up. Click "OK" and then save the file to a location on the local hard drive. The processing should be done locally; do not save to a network location or performance will suffer.

There are some limitations that you must keep in mind. Acrobat has a limit of 10,000 e-mails per conversion, so if you have a large volume of e-mail to process, you must break them down into smaller subsets. It takes time for the conversion process to run its course using Acrobat, so be patient. Obviously, the more powerful a computer you have (faster hard drive, more RAM, and faster processing speed), the quicker you will be able to complete the conversion.

Once the conversion is complete and the portfolio is created, it can be viewed in a flattened or foldered view. The default view is the flattened view showing all e-mails from all folders and recipients. In terms of filtering, you can choose a field to filter, choose operators to apply (e.g., field contains, does not contain, starts with, ends with, etc.), and add search text. You can even have multiple levels of filters (e.g., all messages from John Smith where the subject line contains "Jill" or "Bob" or "Ice Cream"). Files can be marked for privilege and subsequently filtered to remove privileged items prior to production. The layout of the portfolio is also customizable.

E-mail attachments are not converted into separate PDF files. Instead, they are embedded in the PDF e-mail message to which they were originally attached in their original format. They can be reviewed using their native application. Once the initial portfolio is created, it can be reviewed, and nonresponsive or privileged items can be deleted and a subset portfolio can be created to produce to the other side. It is also possible to convert the portfolio to a PDF Binder, which is a single PDF document with multiple pages including attachments. You can export the portfolio list to Excel so you can generate a spreadsheet report. Finally, take a look at EverMap's AutoPortfolio plug-in that, for an additional modest cost, can be used for more robust management of Portfolio files.

At the time this book was written, the cost of Adobe Acrobat X from the Adobe Web site was $449 as a new purchase and $199 as an upgrade of an existing license.

CHAPTER THIRTEEN

Working with Electronic Records at Mediation, Arbitration, or Trial

AT THE END OF the day, after you have gathered all of your electronic records, analyzed them, and determined which are truly relevant, you must be able to use them to help bring about some resolution to the litigation in which you are involved. Whether it is in mediation, arbitration, or trial, you must have a method of displaying the ESI you have determined is relevant to your case. One of the advantages of working with records in electronic format is that they are easy to use with a variety of trial presentation software solutions. Using a laptop or an iPad, either by themselves or with a projector, you have multiple options available for presenting electronic evidence at a very affordable cost. You can easily make a presentation in a conference room or in a courtroom with a minimum amount of equipment. The option you choose will depend on the level of sophistication you want available while making the presentation. Simple solutions exist for presenting static images with software you probably already have. More elaborate presentation techniques, like live highlighting and annotation of documents, zooming in on a section of a document, or creating call outs from documents, are available with products designed specifically for trial presentation purposes.

Before we turn to specific presentation software options, there is a tool you should be aware of that can be used to create screen captures of any ESI you are able to view on your computer monitor or laptop screen.

Snagit from Techsmith is a tool everyone should have on his or her computer. Consider it to be a Print Screen feature on steroids. It works in both Mac and Windows environments and costs only $49.95 for a single-user license. It lets you copy and convert whatever is on your desktop to a standalone image that can then be used in a variety of ways with multiple trial presentation options. You can copy the full desktop view or use other settings to capture only a selected active window or a designated portion or zone of the document you want to copy. You can create a preview version of the screen capture or copy to a clipboard and then insert what you have copied directly into another document. You can also convert what you have copied directly into a PDF document. You can even capture Web pages, static or scrolling, and convert them to PDF files. There are many more advanced features available to enhance the captures that you make, but the basics alone make Snagit a must-have utility.

The easiest and cheapest presentation option is to use something you undoubtedly already have. Obviously you can launch a document in its native application, but that can be cumbersome if you have ESI in multiple formats. You could use Quick View Plus as a presentation tool; it would enable you to navigate a mixed format collection of ESI. However, it does not have a formal presentation view, and you would be limited to viewing the documents in the built-in viewer. Another easy option is to convert everything to PDF and use Adobe Acrobat to present the documents. You can combine all of your documents into one large PDF file and use the thumbnail pane to navigate between exhibits. You can then go to the full-screen view to view the documents in a more presentation-friendly format. You will have the ability to work with the documents using the built-in annotation tools available in Acrobat.

Another option is to use something you likely already own. Microsoft PowerPoint is typically part of your Office suite and available for your use. PowerPoint can be used to create a slideshow of the materials you want to present. Using Snagit in combination with PowerPoint makes the creation of slideshows a simple process. For maximum effectiveness, a dual monitor set up is recommended, although not required. If you use dual monitors, you can have one monitor devoted to viewing the images you want added to the slideshow and the other monitor running PowerPoint. It is then a simple process to open the documents you are interested in, in whatever review tool you are using, and capture them using Snagit. Use the "Save To Clipboard" option in Snagit, and then open a blank slide in

PowerPoint. Click on the slide to give it focus, right click on "Paste," and then size the image that is dropped onto the slide. That is all it takes to create presentation exhibits from your available ESI. You can then take advantage of all the options PowerPoint offers to annotate, animate, or otherwise enhance the slides.

Although this is a good basic technique, there are some inherent limitations in using PowerPoint. Generally, you must present your materials in a linear fashion, and it is not easy to navigate between disparate slides, unless you use the more advanced PowerPoint technique of creating a master slide with hyperlinked thumbnails of the items you want to display, or unless you use the Presenter View with a computer and a projector so you are using a dual-monitor setup. With the latter option, you can scroll on your desktop to find the slide you want to launch and then launch it from the Presenter screen. Neither option is ideal if you have a large collection of documents, nor can you make live annotations, create cutouts, or zoom while the PowerPoint slides are in presentation mode. If you want more advanced features, then you must look at trial presentation software that is specifically designed to present items in a dynamic fashion.

At the time this book was written, the most popular trial presentation tools for Windows-based computers were TrialDirector 6, Sanction 3, and Visionary 8. TrialDirector 6 will also work well on a Mac in Boot Camp mode. TrialSmart was designed specifically to run on a Mac. With the fast-growing popularity of iPads, new applications are also coming to market. TrialPad, Evidence, and Exhibit A are all presentation programs that run on an iPad. The cost for these programs runs from free to around $800, with the more expensive options offering the most comprehensive set of tools and presentation options.

One of the advantages of using a trial presentation program is that it supports a much larger set of exhibits. You normally have a database structure that you can use to organize your materials. When in presentation mode, you have the option of calling up an exhibit by preassigned exhibit number. This offers maximum flexibility in terms of maneuvering through your collection. In addition, you have the option to annotate, zoom, or create document cutouts on the fly. This allows you to make a dynamic presentation, and you can adapt your techniques on an as-needed basis depending on the way the testimony or presentation is going. Finally, several of the programs allow you to build pretreated presentations where you can take specific documents and move from one annotation or highlight to the next, stepping through the document as needed to make your evidentiary point.

Regardless of which presentation method or program you choose, the fact that you are dealing with documents in electronic form from the outset of discovery makes the use of electronic presentation techniques natural at mediation, arbitration, or trial. These tools help you organize your case materials, move quickly between exhibits, and present them with a punch that the use of printed copies of documents lacks.

CHAPTER FOURTEEN

What Is Next?

WE SEE TWO TRENDS developing in the small case market over the next few years. The first is the ongoing emergence of new products. Why? Because the need exists. In the EDna Challenge, Craig Ball described it as a ". . . fast growing need . . . and a huge emerging market." Entrepreneurs and not existing companies will recognize the new paradigm and meet that need.

What about cases that fall between the EDna budget limit of $1,000 and major litigation like *Pension Committee,* a $550 million case arising out of the liquidation of hedge funds? Are their affordable options to handle e-discovery in the lower end of that spectrum? To answer that question, Tom O'Connor drew up the "Ernie Challenge," with advice from Craig Ball and Browning Marean, senior counsel at DLA Piper. Named for his good friend Ernie Svenson, a solo lawyer with a general practice in New Orleans, this challenge covers those "tweener" cases that fall between the range covered by the EDna Challenge and mega cases suitable for the larger brand-name products that dominate the EDD world.

The Ernie Challenge posited a case with roughly 1 TB of data to collect and a final amount of 200 GBs of data to review, the majority being e-mail, with the balance being various types of financial data. It asked for some form of Web review tool in order to work with the clients' counsel and contract staff in a separate location.

Many of the products named in response to the Ernie Challenge duplicated answers to the EDna Challenge. Some were covered in this book. Products such as Adobe Acrobat and Google Apps can scale up to some degree, whereas new offerings from companies such as IPro and Orange

Legal are specifically set at price points within reach of small case lawyers. Nuix figures prominently in many commentaries for reasonably priced options, as do several of the products mentioned in this book, such as Intella and DWR Pro. The original article, which was posted on the EDD Update blog, as well as all the responses, can be found on the Ernie Challenge blog at **http://theerniechallenge.wordpress.com/**. Periodic review of the responses will help keep you up to date in this ever-evolving area.

Glossary

ASCII: The American Standard Code for Information Interchange (pronounced ass-kee). A character-encoding scheme based on the ordering of the English alphabet used to represent text in computer systems. This seven-bit code was later extended by Microsoft in its ANSI codepages used for native non-Unicode or byte-oriented applications using a graphical user interface on Windows systems. These are now officially called "Windows code pages" because the American National Standards Institute has not standardized any of these code pages. See also "Unicode."

Bibliographic Coding: The entering of objective information such as date, document number, and document type into data fields.

Boolean Search: A search for information using "AND," "OR," and "NOT" commands, such as "Tom but not O'Connor" or "bankruptcy and trustee."

Cache: High-speed memory used to temporarily store frequently accessed information because it can be retrieved faster from memory than from the hard drive.

Compression: A technology that reduces the size of a file.

Computer Forensics: The use of specialized techniques for recovery, authentication, and analysis of computer data, typically of data that might have been deleted or destroyed.

Concept Searching: Maps relationships between each word and every other word in large sets of documents and then associates words based on the context in which they are used. Two techniques can be used to perform concept searches: the use of a manually constructed thesaurus that relates certain words to others, or semantic indexing, which is a fully automated method to show associations among words based, in part, on statistical analysis of the occurrence of proximity of certain words to others.

CSV: Comma-Separated Values. A common method of separating data in columns and rows to export into a database. See also "Load File."

Culling: An umbrella term used to describe the processes used to reduce a large document population. See also "Processing."

Database: A collection of related data entered into individual records consisting of a number of different fields.

Deduplication: The process of removing duplicate records from a collection of data. Often called "dededuping" and associated with "near-duping," or the identification of repetitive or iterative documents, such as e-mail conversations, which are not completely identical.

De-NISTing: National Institute of Standards and Technology. A nonregulatory federal agency within the U.S. Department of Commerce that maintains the NSRL, or National Software Reference Library, which identifies software from various sources and can be used to review and match files on a computer. Examples are the program files for applications like Word, Windows, or Excel, which can then be safely removed from a data collection before searches begin.

Deleted Data: Data that once existed on a computer and has subsequently been deleted by the user. Deleted data actually remains on the computer until it is overwritten by new data or "wiped" with a specific software program. (Even after wiping, metadata such as directory entries or pointers might still remain.)

Deleted File: A deleted file that is on disk space designated as available for reuse. The deleted file remains present until it has been overwritten with a new file.

Disk Mirroring: In data storage, the replication of logical disk volumes onto separate physical hard disks in real time to ensure continuous availability. A mirrored volume is a complete logical representation of separate volume copies. The phrase is often misused to mean a forensic image.

Distributed Data: Information that resides on nonlocal devices, such as home computers, laptop computers, PDAs, or even Internet repositories.

ESI: Electronically Stored Information. There is no formal definition ESI in the Federal Rules of Civil Procedure, although Rule 34(a)(1)(A) does provide that a party may serve on any other party a request within the scope of Rule 26(b) to produce "any designated documents or electronically stored information—*including writings, drawings, graphs, charts, photo-*

graphs, sound recordings, images, and other data or data compilations—stored in any medium from which information can be obtained either directly or, if necessary, after translation by the responding party into a reasonably usable form. . . ."

Flat File Database: A database with all data in a single list, similar to a telephone book or a Rolodex.

Forensic Copy: An exact bit-by-bit copy of the entire physical hard drive of a computer system, including slack and unallocated space.

Fragmented Data: "Live" data that has been broken up and stored in various locations on a single hard drive. Most files are stored this way.

Fuzzy Searching: A search that locates words closely matching the spelling of the primary word.

Hash Value: Also known as checksum for a file, this is a value something like a fingerprint of the file. The MD5 hash and SHA-1 are very popular in forensic circles and allow an easy calculation of the value of files which can then be used for comparing or identifying files. The possibility of getting two identical hashes for two different files is so low mathematically as to be considered realistically impossible.

Image: As distinct from document imaging, this refers to making an identical copy of a hard drive. Also known as a "mirror image" or "mirroring."

Load File: A text file with entries for application information and comments. Typically used in ALS to carry instructions about a document image collection for linking to a database program.

Metadata: Information about data that describes how, when, and by whom it was received, created, accessed, and/or modified and how it is formatted. Some metadata is visible, such as file size and date of creation; most is not visible even when the document is printed.

Native File Format: A document produced in the format in which it was originally created.

Objective Coding: The recording of basic data, such as date, author, or document type, from documents into a database.

OCR: Optical Character Recognition. Software that, in conjunction with a scanner, is able to "recognize" written text and convert it to an ASCII file or import it into a word processor so it may perform one of the full-text searches.

PDF: Portable Document Format. From Adobe, it is used as a standard for document exchange.

Processing: Typically the culling, deduping, and de-NISTing procedure used by an e-discovery vendor, but definitions vary widely from vendor to vendor.

PST: Personal Storage Table. A local download off the Exchange Server store of a user's e-mail, contacts, calendar, and folder structure information. The PST file can be exported and thus used for producing e-mail. It is often confused with the OST file, which Outlook creates automatically as an exact replica of a user mailbox on the Exchange Server, and which the user can access when offline from the Exchange Server.

Relational Database: A database containing records in fields that are somehow connected or "related." This allows simultaneous searches of multiple fields.

Residual Data: Data that is not active on a computer system, such as data in media-free space, slack space, or in files that have been "deleted." Sometimes called Ambient Data.

Sampling: The process of statistically testing data for the presence of relevant information. Often used to provide courts with a cost estimate in order to allocate cost sharing.

Service Bureau: A vendor that performs ALS services such as photo-copying, scanning, imaging, coding and, more recently, e-discovery services.

Slack Space: The difference between the size of a file and the size of the various clusters where it is stored because the file segments might be smaller than the clusters where they reside. May also refer to data fragments stored randomly on a hard drive during the normal operation of a computer or residual data left on a hard drive after new data has overwritten deleted files.

Spoliation: The original legal definition was the destruction of a thing by the act of a stranger, as in the erasure or alteration of a writing by the act of a stranger. In e-discovery cases, the focus has been on the intentional nature of the act, which can include deletion, partial destruction, or alteration generally by a party to the action or someone under the party's control.

Subjective Coding: Entering information from a document that requires the coder to exercise judgment, such as subject or issue codes. This field often is left blank for the law firm's paralegals or associates to fill in.

TIFF: Tagged Image File Format. A data format used to render an electronic image of a document and commonly used by most service bureaus in their scanning process. See also "PDF."

Unicode: A computing industry standard for encoding and handling text from most of the world's writing systems. Developed by the nonprofit Unicode Consortium, it contains more than 109,000 separate characters and character encodings. Simply put, it uses one byte for any ASCII characters, which have the same code values in both Unicode and ASCII encoding, and up to four bytes for other characters. Its goal is to replace existing character encoding schemes such as ASCII and ANSI (sic) with unifying character sets, and it has been implemented in many recent technologies, including XML, the Java programming language, the Microsoft .NET Framework, and modern operating systems.

XML: Extensible Markup Language. Defines a set of rules for encoding documents in a format that is both human-readable and machine-readable. It is designed to facilitate the exchange of documents and is used widely in modern Internet applications.

Index

Find Info Like a Pro, Volume 2: Mining the Internet's Public Records for Investigative Research
By Carole A. Levitt and Mark E. Rosch

Product Code: 5110709 / LPM Price: $47.95 / Regular Price: $79.95

Don't waste time and money on hiring someone to do your investigative research when you can do it yourself. The second volume in this important series focuses on public records that are filed and stored with government agencies, which are accessible for public inspection. The authors address both paid and unpaid resources on the Internet.

Google for Lawyers: Essential Search Tips and Productivity Tools
By Carole A. Levitt and Mark E. Rosch

Product Code: 5110704 / LPM Price: $47.95 / Regular Price: $79.95

This book introduces novice Internet searchers to the diverse collection of information locatable through Google. The book discusses the importance of including effective Google searching as part of a lawyer's due diligence, and cites case law that mandates that lawyers should use Google and other resources available on the Internet, where applicable. For intermediate and advanced users, the book unlocks the power of various advanced search strategies and hidden search features they might not be aware of.

The Lawyer's Guide to Microsoft Outlook 2010
By Ben M. Schorr

Product Code: 5110720 / LPM Price: $41.95 / Regular Price: $69.95

Outlook is the most used application in Microsoft Office, but are you using it to your greatest advantage? The Lawyer's Guide to Microsoft® Outlook 2010 is the only guide written specifically for lawyers to help you be more productive, more efficient and more successful. More than just email, Outlook is also a powerful task, contact, and scheduling manager that will improve your practice. From helping you log and track phone calls, meetings, and correspondence to archiving closed case material in one easy-to-store location, this book unlocks the secrets of "underappreciated" features that you will use every day. Written in plain language by a twenty-year veteran of law office technology and ABA member, this book will help you:

- Sort and group messages to de-clutter your inbox
- Find old e-mails quickly
- Create an effective to-do list
- Master your calendar
- Work with journal entries
- Add, organize, and share contacts
- Utilize long-term storage when you're done with a case or client
- Back up your data
- Track and log phone calls, meetings, and correspondence
- Take advantage of time-saving keyboard shortcuts

The Electronic Evidence and Discovery Handbook: Forms, Checklists, and Guidelines
By Sharon D. Nelson, Bruce A. Olson, and John W. Simek

Product Code: 5110569 / LPM Price: $99.95 / Regular Price: $129.95

The use of electronic evidence has increased dramatically over the past few years, but many lawyers still struggle with the complexities of electronic discovery. This substantial book provides lawyers with the templates they need to frame their discovery requests and provides helpful advice on what they can subpoena. In addition to the ready-made forms, the authors also supply explanations to bring you up to speed on the electronic discovery field. The accompanying CD-ROM features over 70 forms, including, Motions for Protective Orders, Preservation and Spoliation Documents, Motions to Compel, Electronic Evidence Protocol Agreements, Requests for Production, Internet Services Agreements, and more. Also included is a full electronic evidence case digest with over 300 cases detailed!

The 2012 Solo and Small Firm Legal Technology Guide
By Sharon D. Nelson, Esq., John W. Simek, and Michael C. Maschke

Product Code: 5110730 / LPM Price: $54.95 / Regular Price: $89.95

This annual guide is the only one of its kind written to help solo and small firm lawyers find the best technology for their dollar. You'll find the most current information and recommendations on computers, servers, networking equipment, legal software, printers, security products, smart phones, and anything else a law office might need. It's written in clear, easily understandable language to make implementation simpler if you choose to do it yourself, or you can use it in conjunction with your IT consultant. Either way, you'll learn how to make technology work for you.

LinkedIn in One Hour for Lawyers
By Dennis Kennedy and Allison C. Shields

Product Code: 5110737 / LPM Price: $19.95 / Regular Price: $34.95

Lawyers work in a world of networks, connections, referrals, and recommendations. For many lawyers, the success of these networks determines the success of their practice. LinkedIn®, the premier social networking tool for business, can help you create, nurture, and expand your professional network and gain clients in the process. LinkedIn® in One Hour for Lawyers provides an introduction to this powerful tool in terms that any attorney can understand. In just one hour, you will learn to:

- Set up a LinkedIn account
- Complete your basic profile
- Create a robust, dynamic profile that will attract clients
- Build your connections
- Use search tools to enhance your network
- Maximize your presence with features such as groups, updates, answers, and recommendations
- Monitor your network with ease
- Optimize your settings for privacy concerns
- Use LinkedIn® effectively in the hiring process
- Develop a LinkedIn strategy to grow your legal network

Virtual Law Practice:
How to Deliver Legal Services Online
By Stephanie L. Kimbro

Product Code: 5110707 / LPM Price: $47.95 / Regular Price: $79.95

The legal market has recently experienced a dramatic shift as lawyers seek out alternative methods of practicing law and providing more affordable legal services. Virtual law practice is revolutionizing the way the public receives legal services and how legal professionals work with clients. If you are interested in this form of practicing law, *Virtual Law Practice* will help you:

- *Responsibly deliver legal services online to* your clients
- Successfully set up and operate a virtual law office
- Establish a virtual law practice online through a secure, client-specific portal
- Manage and market your virtual law practice
- Understand state ethics and advisory opinions
- Find more flexibility and work/life balance in the legal profession

The Lawyer's Essential Guide to Writing
By Marie Buckley

Product Code: 5110726 / LPM Price: $47.95 / Regular Price: $79.95

This is a readable, concrete guide to contemporary legal writing. Based on Marie Buckley's years of experience coaching lawyers, this book provides a systematic approach to all forms of written communication, from memoranda and briefs to e-mail and blogs. The book sets forth three principles for powerful writing and shows how to apply those principles to develop a clean and confident style.

iPad in One Hour for Lawyers
By Tom Mighell

Product Code: 5110719 / LPM Price: $19.95 / Regular Price: $34.95

Whether you are a new or a more advanced iPad user, *iPad in One Hour for Lawyers* takes a great deal of the mystery and confusion out of using your iPad. Ideal for lawyers who want to get up to speed swiftly, this book presents the essentials so you don't get bogged down in technical jargon and extraneous features and apps. In just six, short lessons, you'll learn how to:

- Quickly Navigate and Use the iPad User Interface
- Set Up Mail, Calendar, and Contacts
- Create and Use Folders to Multitask and Manage Apps
- Add Files to Your iPad, and Sync Them
- View and Manage Pleadings, Case Law, Contracts, and other Legal Documents
- Use Your iPad to Take Notes and Create Documents
- Use Legal-Specific Apps at Trial or in Doing Research

iPad Apps in One Hour for Lawyers
By Tom Mighell

Product Code: 5110739 / LPM Price: $19.95 / Regular Price: $34.95

At last count, there were more than 80,000 apps available for the iPad. Finding the best apps often can be an overwhelming, confusing, and frustrating process. iPad Apps in One Hour for Lawyers provides the "best of the best" apps that are essential for any law practice. In just one hour, you will learn about the apps most worthy of your time and attention. This book will describe how to buy, install, and update iPad apps, and help you:

- Find apps to get organized and improve your productivity
- Create, manage, and store documents on your iPad
- Choose the best apps for your law office, including litigation and billing apps
- Find the best news, reading, and reference apps
- Take your iPad on the road with apps for travelers
- Maximize your social networking power
- Have some fun with game and entertainment apps during your relaxation time

How to Start and Build a Law Practice,
Platinum Fifth Edition
By Jay G Foonberg

Product Code: 5110508 / LPM Price: $57.95 / Regular Price: $69.95

This classic ABA bestseller has been used by tens of thousands of lawyers as the comprehensive guide to planning, launching, and growing a successful practice. It's packed with over 600 pages of guidance on identifying the right location, finding clients, setting fees, managing your office, maintaining an ethical and responsible practice, maximizing available resources, upholding your standards, and much more. You'll find the information you need to successfully launch your practice, run it at maximum efficiency, and avoid potential pitfalls along the way. If you're committed to starting—and growing—your own practice, this one book will give you the expert advice you need to make it succeed for years to come.

Social Media for Lawyers: The Next Frontier
By Carolyn Elefant and Nicole Black

Product Code: 5110710 / LPM Price: $47.95 / Regular Price: $79.95

The world of legal marketing has changed with the rise of social media sites such as Linkedin, Twitter, and Facebook. Law firms are seeking their companies attention with tweets, videos, blog posts, pictures, and online content. Social media is fast and delivers news at record pace. This book provides you with a practical, goal-centric approach to using social media in your law practice that will enable you to identify social media platforms and tools that fit your practice and implement them easily, efficiently, and ethically.

30-DAY RISK-FREE ORDER FORM

Please print or type. To ship UPS, we must have your street address. If you list a P.O. Box, we will ship by U.S. Mail.

Name _____

Member ID _____

Firm/Organization _____

Street Address _____

City/State/Zip _____

Area Code/Phone (In case we have a question about your order) _____

E-mail _____

Method of Payment:

❑ Check enclosed, payable to American Bar Association
❑ MasterCard   ❑ Visa   ❑ American Express

Card Number _____ Expiration Date _____

Signature Required _____

MAIL THIS FORM TO:
American Bar Association, Publication Orders
P.O. Box 10892, Chicago, IL 60610

ORDER BY PHONE:
24 hours a day, 7 days a week:
Call 1-800-285-2221 to place a credit card order.
We accept Visa, MasterCard, and
American Express.

EMAIL ORDERS: orders@americanbar.org
FAX: 1-312-988-5568

VISIT OUR WEB SITE: www.ShopABA.org
Allow 7-10 days for regular UPS delivery. Need it
sooner? Ask about our overnight delivery options.
Call the ABA Service Center at 1-800-285-2221
for more information.

GUARANTEE:
If—for any reason—you are not satisfied with your
purchase, you may return it within 30 days of
receipt for a refund of the price of the book(s).
No questions asked.

Thank You For Your Order.

Join the ABA Law Practice Management Section today and receive a substantial discount on Section publications!

Product Code:	Description:	Quantity:	Price:	Total Price:
				$
				$
				$
				$
				$

		Subtotal: $
*Tax: IL residents add 9.5% DC residents add 6%		*Tax: $
		**Shipping/Handling: $
Yes, I am an ABA member and would like to join the Law Practice Management Section today! (Add $50.00)		$
		Total: $

**Shipping/Handling:

$0.00 to $9.99	add $0.00
$10.00 to $49.99	add $5.95
$50.00 to $99.99	add $7.95
$100.00 to $199.99	add $9.95
$200.00 to $499.99	add $12.95